Have We Met Before?

Emma Belle Donath

ISBN-10: 0-86690-036-5
ISBN-13: 978-0-86690-036-2

Cover Design: Jack Cipolla

Published by:
American Federation of Astrologers, Inc.
6535 S. Rural Road
Tempe, AZ 85283

www.astrologers.com

Printed in the United States of America

Contents

Contents

Foreword

It is an honor and a pleasure to introduce Emma Belle
Donath's new boook, *Have We Met Before?* In recent years
those of us who have been counseling others have discovered
that often the real core of a person's problem may not be
found to have its origin in this lifetime. This is at least the
way that the person perceives his or her situation. As a result
of this discovery and the recent finding of more and more evidence to support a belief in reincarnation, many of us in the
counseling and guidance fields have added to our resources
for helping our clients the therapeutic tool of Past Lives
Therapy. In certain cases this therapeutic technique has
proved most effective. I have personally used this form of
therapy numerous times when it appeared that it could help
the client deal with the reality of today by having a better understanding of the past.

In this book, which focuses on analyzing the natal horoscope
in relation to past lives, the author has provided still another
tool for the past-life therapist. Using her vast knowledge and
astrological skills she has presented in a very readable and
understandable form some guidelines as to where we have
been in the past, who we were, and how these events in the
past may be linked to our present lives. The author has done

this in such a way that even those uninitiated in astrology can understand and profit from reading this book.

For those who are knowledgeable in astrology, her book becomes a valid and important tool in the practice of their work. For the past-life therapist, it should become must reading and for the individual who wishes to expand his or her knowledge in the areas of astrology and reincarnation, this work can be a point of embarkation for new and exciting experiences. I am excited about what I have found on the pages of *Have We Met Before?* and I am sure that once you have read it, you will share my excitement.

James E. Swain, Ph. D.
President, National Self-Awareness Institute

Director of Mental Health for Preble Co., Ohio

Whatsoever a man soweth,
that shall he also reap.

Past Lives:
Fact or Fiction?

Reincarnation is described in the dictionary as "giving a new body to the soul." There has been a revival of debate about the occurrences of past lives, and major religions in the Eastern countries predominantly encourage the acceptance of various forms of reincarnation while the Western world yet holds this belief at bay. Although there have been many documents written pro and con on this premise, the more influential religious denominations have made no moves to re-evaluate the Roman Catholic decisions of the sixth century to deny validity of this canon.

However, such renowned philosophers as Goethe, John Donne, William Blake, St. Augustine, A. Conan Doyle, Leslie Weatherhead, Benjamin Franklin, lames A. Pike, Thomas Carlyle, Mark Twain, H. G. Wells, Nevil Shute, lack London, David Lloyd George, Rudolf Steiner, and Leo Tolstoy have accepted the concept of a continuity of spirit from one physical body to another. Steiner even went so far as to state that the whole future of the planet Earth depends upon how men have lived in their previous incarnations.

Throughout historical times, various religious doctrines have included a thread to help unravel this mystery about continuing lives. The Animism of early tribal groups, including the Amer-Indians, taught that all objects have a spirit or ghost that leaves when the body dies and attaches itself to someone else or something else. In this vein, the killing of a brave hunter would enable one to inherit his fearless soul. From the Native Americans comes the idea of a rabbit as a symbol of resurrection, presently utilized at the Easter season.

Ancient Egyptians pictured the spirit, or "ba," leaving the body as a tiny bird above the mouth of the corpse. In this manner the living soul winged its flight away from the dead physical body.

Both Buddhist and Hindu priests of the Asian countries have long declared the complicated stages toward Nirvana. There are many levels through which one must pass in successive lives on a pathway to enlightenment. From these teachers comes our present concept of karma, or the law of action and reaction.

During the beginning of the Christian Era, the two major Jewish sects were diametrically opposed in their views about reincarnation. The Sadducees rejected any ideas of an afterlife, while the Pharisees taught various theories about the soul after death. In the past few decades since the unearthing of the Dead Sea Scrolls, some of the teachings of a rather obscure esoteric sect called the Essenes have come to light and give further credence to a more metaphysical approach during that time period. As with all biblical sections, scholars today differ about the true interpretation of the portions of the texts that indicate an acceptance of life after death.

2

Jewish cabalists of the Middle Ages penned an intricate system of principles concerning the origin of the universe and the original separation of individual souls from the love and security of God. These precepts are being eagerly sought by today's students of the occult.

In the beginning centuries of its existence, the concept of reincarnation was openly accepted by the Roman Catholic Church, but through various stages and political maneuvering from the fourth century onward through the suppression of the Cathars, this belief in the continuity of the spirit has been denied arid suppressed. Persons expressing an idea of previous existences received the full brunt of punishment during the Spanish Inquisition.

Within the present scope of interest concerning past lives, several theories have evolved and are prevailing. Death in one body, followed by being reborn as an infant to grow and develop through another period of childhood, adolescence, and maturity, is the most widely accepted idea. This pattern is determined by the karmic lessons that are to be met and conquered, as well as the karmic relationships through which earlier injustices are to be worked out during a particular time period. The incarnating soul or spirit is aware of past problems and opportunities, but the conscious awareness of the personality is oblivious of such patterns until it reaches a certain depth of perception. Analysis of dreams, communing with the subconscious, regression through meditation or hypnosis, and other methods of raising the awareness are ways of reaching this level of understanding. The individual aim is to erase all evil karma in order to return to the perfection of unity with God or the Cosmic Creator.

Because there was found such similarity between occurrences from one previous life to another, various therapists began to consider the possibility of presently living throughout simultaneous time periods. Some writers have described this as being on a boat floating down a sharply winding river of time, yet being able to see across an S-shaped curve into another segment at once. Other metaphysicians have considered this as a multi-tiered cake which, when cut, will expose several layers of crumbs and frosting. Science fiction writers have speculated about characters residing in the same areas, yet living in such different frames of time and space as to be completely unrelated. So, one current concept of multiple lives considers the soul to be alive today as well as yesterday and tomorrow all at once. Therefore, each action in one life would have a reaction in every other existence.

One concept involves the oversoul, or chairman, of the incarnating souls. Each personal soul is like a student in the classroom of an oversoul who periodically checks up on his or her charges and evaluates their progress. Therefore, each individual may be affected to some degree by the activity of his or her fellow students.

One of the earlier theories about continuing consciousness was the genetic pool or the ability to communicate with a cosmic consciousness into which all earthly information and action is fed and contained. During the life period, a man or woman is free to tap this resource in order to share knowledge or skills gained in the past. Some geneticists have carried this idea a step further in suggesting that the reproductive cells contain chemical memories of all the forebearers of that particular individual.

4

Some regression specialists are presently espousing the idea of parallel souls, wherein an individual soul has split itself into two or more sections inhabiting several bodies during the same time period. In this manner these twin spirits may work through more karmic conditions than would be possible in one body.

In some cases where individuals have endured near death experiences, there seems to have been an exchange of souls inhabiting that particular physical vehicle. Renowned author Ruth Montgomery has written extensively about the concept, terming the entering soul a "walk in." The explanation seems to be a mutually agreed upon opportunity to complete limited karmic lessons without again going through the periods of childhood and adolescence.

Many counselors are today using one or more of these concepts of reincarnation in order to assist people to find the core of their physical and psychological problems. These techniques are by no means limited to astrologers, mediums, and spiritualists, but are being widely employed by psychologists, hypnotists, theologians, and marriage therapists. Myriad volumes are available in libraries and bookstores describing the beneficial effects of such therapy. For, as Rudolf Steiner explained, it is only by eliminating the past and concentrating on the present that we may go forward. All subconscious fears and blocks must be brought forth and vanquished before the soul can travel to spiritual enlightenment.

In some small way the analysis of the natal horoscope with consideration of past lives in mind may be of added assistance in helping the client learn more about himself or herself.

Comparing Charts

Among the various methods used to look at relationships through astrology is a technique called chart comparison or synastry. The astrology of relationships can lead to a deeper understanding of the native, plus the subconscious reactions of other people. Synastry is both the conscious and unconscious reaction of two or more persons to each other in any given situation. Knowledge of these reactions, whether automatic or deliberate, should help each of the individuals be more responsible for their own personal responses and actions. Seeing into another's inner emotions and motivations through the natal horoscope gives personal empathy in understanding how their alliance affects each one, both separately and together.

In looking at the natal horoscope to find past lives together, a simple procedure is followed. In fact these techniques may be followed even if the precise birth time is unknown for either or both persons involved.

Follow these simple steps:
1. Erect the natal horoscopes in your usual manner.

2. Set up an Aries-rising, equal-house chart using zero degrees of each zodiacal sign on its natural house cusp.

3. Then place the planets of one natal horoscope into the inner ring of the Aries-rising chart.

4. Then place the planets of the other native into the outer circle of the Aries-rising chart.

5. Now draw a line through each pair of planets that are conjunct from person A's horoscope to person B's horoscope. Use an orb of only five degrees for these comparison conjunctions.

7. If one planet in either horoscope is conjunct two or more planets in the other horoscope, draw as many lines as necessary,

8. Next read the following chapters to determine which past incarnations between these two individuals are influencing this particular life period.

In Chart 1, the following planets are considered to be effective in the karmic comparison:

Male	to	Female	in	Sign
Sun	to	Moon	in	Pisces
Vesta	to	Moon	in	Pisces
Vesta	to	Vesta	in	Pisces
Moon	to	Vesta	in	Pisces
Mercury	to	Vesta	in	Pisces
Jupiter	to	Saturn	in	Leo
Jupiter	to	Pluto	in	Leo
Saturn	to	Ceres	in	Aquarius

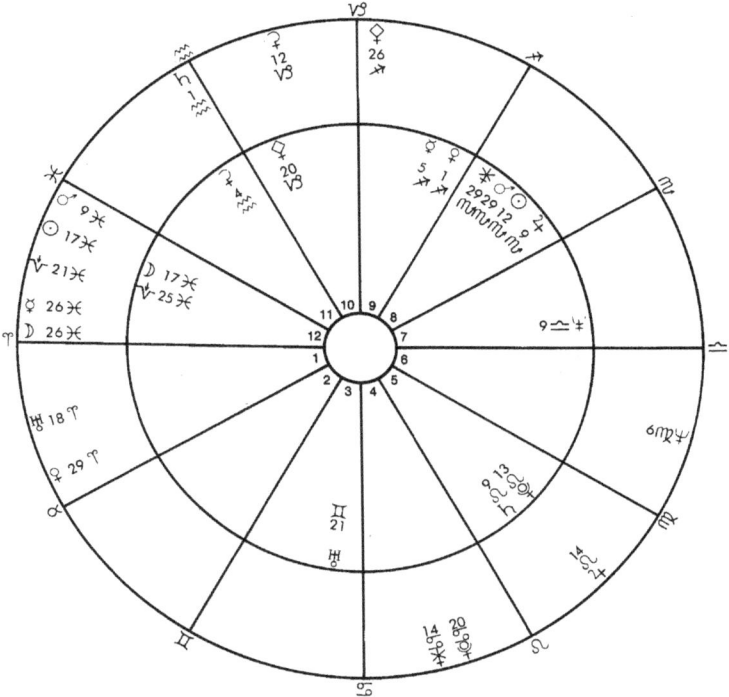

Chart 1. A: inner, female; B: outer, male

9

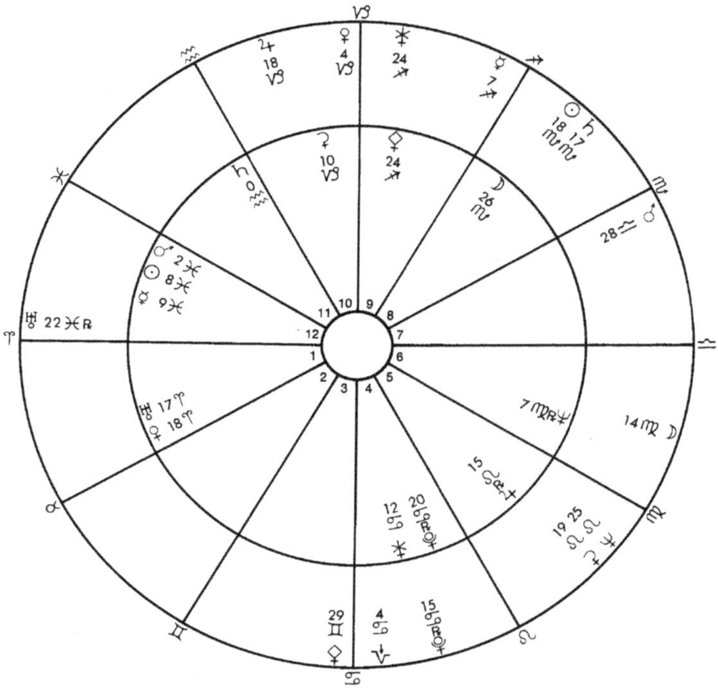

Chart 2. A, inner, female; B, outer, male

In Chart 2, the following planets are considered to be effective in the karmic comparison:

Male	to	Female	in	Sign
Pluto	to	Juno	in	Cancer
Ceres	to	Jupiter	in	Leo
Juno	to	Pallas	in	Sagittarius

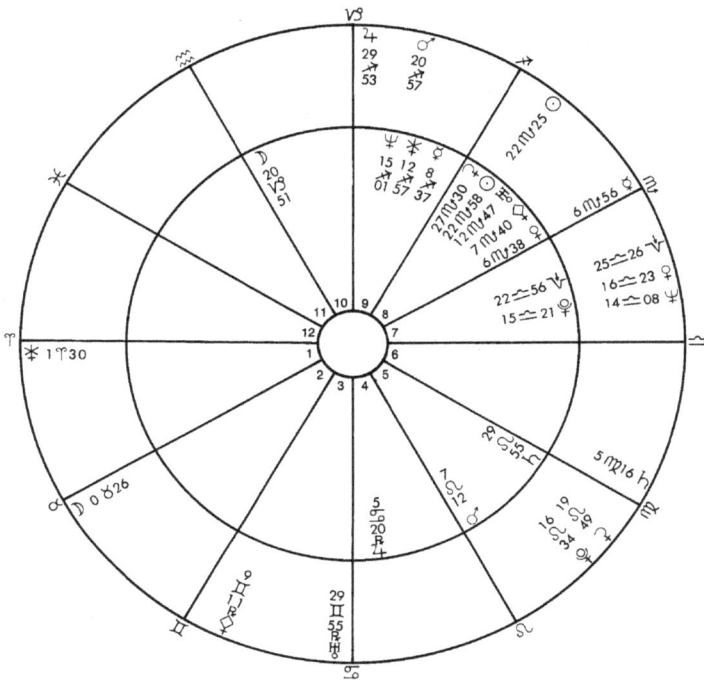

Chart 3. A, inner, nephew; B, outer, uncle

In Chart 3, the following planets are considered to be effective in the karmic comparison:

Uncle	to	Nephew	in	Sign
Neptune	to	Pluto	in	Libra
Venus	to	Pluto	in	Libra
Vesta	to	Vesta	in	Libra
Mercury	to	Venus	in	Scorpio
Sun	to	Sun	in	Scorpio
Sun	to	Ceres	in	Scorpio
Mars	to	Neptune	in	Sagittarius

11

Where Were We?

Whatever memories are evoked by past lives are only valid in counseling or evaluating a relationship as they aid and assist the individuals concerned to adjust to the present life with its separate environment and lessons. No attempt should ever be made to help people actually return to past situations or to past time periods. That time and location are finished and may only be used to understand the present. Evolution is an ongoing process and people have been given the many tools at hand to help them proceed on the journey forward. The times and places given for the various signs of the zodiac are merely those that have been found meaningful for experimental horoscopes of clients. Rather than the actual age or culture described, the memories may have only been suggestive of that type of social structure.

A variety of examples from actual horoscopes of clients (without names or birth dates) are presented here. In each case the particular situation has been helpful to the two individuals involved in explaining their present relationship. Sometimes there is an adjustment necessary because of the present conditions, while at other times this explanation merely enhances an otherwise pleasant association.

Aries

The primary focus of planets in Aries seems to be related to lives led during the tribal days of early Canaan and Palestine. This affinity with early Hebrew nomadic life shows up in the need to either be a very strong, dogmatic leader or to look for someone like that to follow. There is a need to excel in some type of work or sports. Fighting at the drop of the hat, answering a challenge with positive action, living in large family units that are dominated by a single leader, looking up to a champion, or being completely submissive to a master are typical of the sub-conscious reactions of this particular placement.

When a young woman client met a certain older couple, her memories were stirred to think about a nomadic life on the arid sands of what is now called Saudi Arabia. Not the man, but the older woman, had been her companion during that past lifetime when both women had shared a common husband. In other words, the two women had been members of the same harem.

During prehistoric days in Africa, the aforementioned young woman had lured another friend into leaving home in search of fabled wild game. During the course of the hunt, both men (for both individuals were in the male body in early Africa) were killed and never returned home to their waiting families. This young woman is presently leery of permanent ties.

A present day father and son who enjoy an unusual rapport in spite of their age difference were found to have shared a common life as co-counselors for a rugged Scottish chieftain. Truly this was a life of hardship, but one where the two men developed a long lasting mutual understanding.

The reversal of the sexual roles is not unusual; neither is the reversal of parental circumstance. A present day mother and daughter were also child and parent trekking across the desert with the patriarch Moses during the Exodus out of Egypt. During that early life, the mother cared for a delicate daughter during hot and rugged days. Now the once weak child is the strong and nurturing mother figure.

Taurus
Living close to nature is meaningful to these natives from early childhood because of time during a past life spent on a farm or in natural surroundings. There is an affinity with the area around the Mediterranean Sea and with ancient Egypt. The entire Near East lived in this manner in earlier days as did the Amer-Indians of North and South America before Columbus sailed west. Farming and hunting are familiar life-styles even if this extends only to keeping flowers in tubs or boxes in an urban apartment. There is greater confidence in natural or herbal healing methods than in sophisticated technology. Women were more feminine, yet more respected during these times than in the present age. There are some Oriental overtones, especially of ancient China, called Cathay.

A present day father-son relationship was found to have existed before, but in the times when the Illinois Native Americans roamed the banks of the Wabash River in southern Ohio and Indiana. These two men were born in another country during this century, but immigrated to the American midwest in search of this former home. Together or apart, they both draw strength and peace from being in the countryside.

Life as a woman in ancient Cathay comes to the surface for a certain young woman when she relates closely with her young son. With this child she prefers the use of native herbs to heal his minor ills. Because of a past life when she soothed and humored her then lord and master, she tends to spoil her now young child.

The peaceful manner in which a couple accept minor and major setbacks goes back over several centuries to a life they shared on a rocky farm in southern Italy. During that past life period, this couple struggled to even feed themselves and their growing family. So today material accumulations are appreciated rather than expected.

Gemini
A life in the Middle Ages is found most often with planets in this moveable sign. There were very set social patterns with men and women having a very definite place in society. French, British, and Germanic lords and ladies on their graceful steeds at the various tournaments show the excitement and adventure associated with the typical Gemini. There was also travel to the Crusades, exchanges with caravan owners going back and forth to China and India, the constant quarreling and visiting among families and neighboring castles—all-in-all, a sense of restlessness that lasts into the present life. In earlier ages, a life on the southern continent of Australia or one of its nearby islands has been found.

Carrying milady's colors into a tourney is not far removed from this present life when a young man brings home his sports trophies for the approval of his present life mother. Certainly this boy's need for favor is as great during the present life as it was during the Age of Chivalry. This boy was once a knight and soldier serving under the woman who was once his lady queen and is now his mother.

A woman who is now a student of a gentle and kindly teacher was once before in this same position. During the past life the student and teacher traveled across the countryside of what was then Germanic city states and castles. As in the past, this woman feels a compulsion to spread the word about her teacher's wisdom to all who will listen. Today, this embarrasses the present life teacher.

During a past time period in tenth-century Britain, a nursemaid cared for a boy child who became a wise and revered priest. In this present life the former nursemaid is now a conscientious young man who has married the woman who was once that boy priest. Now the young man has pledged himself to be devoted and concerned for an invalid wife, showing as much care and love as he did once in the past when their genders were reversed. The man gives validity to the present young woman's philosophies, as he did in the life before. The encouragement and devotion have thus been reestablished in a far different setting and social structure.

Cancer
The Pacific Islands bring back fond memories for many natives with planets in this watery sign. Whether these people lived in relatively recent historical times, or in the distant past of Lernuria, there is an affinity and awe of the element of water. They are happiest living near rather large bodies of water, but sense also the changing barometer when the weather fluctuates. However, there is an understanding of the power of the nature, so there is almost a philosophy of predestination and helplessness about life's events. Many of these lives were rather emotional ones lived during periods when children were reared primarily by the mother or the maternal relatives in accord with local customs. During peri-

ods of stress, there is a tendency to return to the patterns of this early time when the native was not held responsible for his or her actions or shortcomings. This behavior can bring a habit of making excuses for personal action

One couple during this life period was unable to work out their differences. Some of the strain was due to vibrations left over from their lives as an Easter Island queen and her religious advisor or priest. During this century the roles or genders are reversed so that the former priest is now a woman and the former queen is now a man. The sense of dependency proved too much for them to overcome in the present association.

A present life student and teacher were once a husband and wife who built a happy home together. Even though both individuals are female in the present life, there is a strong tie of love and affection. Because of memories of parenting together, they have been helpful to each other in sharing the problems and joys of their present life children. They were together on a long ago Pacific Island where life was peaceful and leisurely.

There were differences in body appearance and density, as well as weight and height, during past times in the Pacific continent of Lemuria, and the soul brings with it such far-flung memories. A student and his teacher remembered such vivid memories and now share dreams of this long ago continent. The boy had once been a maiden who watched over and loved her kingly master. The female teacher had once been a king and master over many subjects including the maiden who is now her young boy student Much understanding and concern are present between these two individuals.

Leo

The courts of the French kings are familiar to these natives as they read historical novels or dream of past grandeurs. There remains the sense of individualism and intrigue to this day. If fewer personal planets are involved by conjunction in this sign, there will have been interest in the great artistic and spiritual work of the magnificent cathedrals that still dot the countryside of this part of the world. In an earlier period the adventuresome Vikings of the Scandinavian shores also loved and lived in the same exciting manner, minus the elaborate trappings of furs and jewels. A far distant vibration reaches from the time of the pyramid builders in the mountains of South America, the plains of Central America, and the then Egyptian plain. There is a sense of dignity and pride remaining that can either hinder or enhance relationships.

Friends who once spent a life in the French royal court are now suburbanites. But their past lives as a titled gentleman and his entitled heir show up from time to time as they plan their occasional pleasures. Dining in fine restaurants complete with silver, flowers, and service delights them.

A teacher who was once a captive queen in Viking days is now assisted by a student who was then her guard and means of escape. During this period in the twentieth century the former guard, now student, helps the woman once again to escape. This time the relief is from the boredom of mundane chores, rather than a Viking warrior.

Living in America today, there are few dangers of being beheaded, but that memory remains for a young woman who experienced such a fate. Her past life husband now associates with her as a friend and mentor. The former husband continues to caution the former wife about inappropriate and foolish actions, as he did in the past in France.

Virgo
Describe a green, fertile valley surrounded by high mountains which cut off the windy gales and snowy blasts so that the temperature is constant throughout the year and these natives will return to that long ago idyllic locale in their dreams. This Green Valley of western Brazil was also known as the home of the mighty Amazon daughters who once roamed the known world and were renowned for their bravery and valor as well as for their fabled healing techniques. Women having planets in this sign are less likely to be willingly suppressed and are normally inclined to shoulder their share of any load. More recent lives may have been during the ages of the Aztec Indians of Mexico, the Holy Crusades of Mecca, or with Alexander on his treks into Arabia and India.

A former soldier serving under Alexander the Great is now an amateur artist living in a small suburban village. She once protected a brave Indian widow, living in the foothills of the Himalaya Mountains from certain death. During this present lifetime both souls have incarnated in the female form and are the best of friends. The former soldier again protects the former widow from all possible harm including a battering husband.

Men, who were once Aztec priest and ritualist, now live in the American midwest as father and son. Their former interest in music forms remains to this day. The knowledge of the physical body has been replaced by an interest in biology of animals. Each retains the courage to make a decisive incision, but this time for healing rather than for sacrifice.

20

When a couple has been man and wife several times during past incarnations, it is difficult for them to relate in any other manner during the present time period. Even though the present day husband is deeply in love with another woman, as well as being sexually attracted to her, he will not consider leaving his legal wife. The present wife accepts such behavior as normal for she too recalls the planned marriage of the Indian culture, far in their shared past. Their rather platonic relationship in no way hinders their efficient way of running a business together during present times. All affairs are in the husband's name even though the wife handles most of the day-to-day business. They are content with that arrangement because it seems proper to the two individuals involved.

Libra
Although scarcely recognized in modern history books, the sub-continent of India has been home to flourishing civilizations throughout history. As man's scientific knowledge waxes and wanes over the centuries, a country's economic growth increases or slows. As man's spiritual development keeps him in a state of contemplation, the country often is left in the hands of less ethical rulers and politicians. So has been the history of that great land mass. With planets in this sign of duality, people may remember times of great artists, sculptors, poets, and craftsmen of ancient India as well as the more recent leaders of prosperous, classical Greece. Even latter day Venice, Florence, and other Italian cities developed some of this love of beauty and appreciation of the artisan. That which is crass and primitive will be difficult for these natives to accept gracefully. There were many of these individuals incarnated in the southern states of the United States immediately before the Civil War. Now these people must learn the lesson of providing for their own luxury and com-

fort rather than to enslave others to perform their necessary chores.

Two female friends who are involved in the same professional activities find themselves to have the closeness normally found only between family members. This is not surprising because they were actually sisters during a past life in Greece. Memories of exciting days in Athens during the time of the classical philosophers spurs them both on to constant bouts of learning about new facts and theories.

A young man and woman who were once teacher and pupil find their roles reversed during the present incarnation. The former teacher is yet in the male physical body, but now learns about art and beauty from his present wife, who was the former student. The young wife is an interior decorator in the present time period.

It is no wonder that a suburban mother leans heavily on her older son for mental and emotional support. During a long ago past period in the sophisticated cultural centers of eastern Italy, the present son was the spiritual advisor to the present mother and her family. During the course of that incarnation the woman was widowed while her children were yet small and she leaned heavily on the young priest for advice and comfort.

Scorpio
Both the once mighty Tartars and the culturally sophisticated Chinese have a common trait of being able to perform what is necessary without being debilitated by personal emotions. The Chinese lady who bore countless children, organized and ran a household and charmed her lord and master while

bearing the constant pain of broken, strapped feet never allowed herself a senseless moan or groan about her fate in life as did the Mongol soldier fighting to death without pause for injury or pain. They learned to deal with life as it unfolded without waste of energy for personal considerations. There are threads of this energy found in more recent incarnations among the plains Native Americans. Because of this suppressing of individual feelings, planets in this sign may seem to be cold and uncaring when they are really filled with true compassion. There is also an acquired dignity in this contact.

The Grand Canal from Soochow to Peking, China, once carried the supplies of grain to this northern capital city in order to feed the multitudes then living in the northern areas of this great Asian country. No one would remember this more clearly than a present day man and woman who once lived there under different guises. The present life man was once advisor and counselor to the war lord who governed that Eastern Province of ancient Cathay. The woman in this incarnation was once the war lord who governed at ancient Suzhou, or Soochow, as it is now known.

A child who was reared by a Byzantine nun in old Constantinople is now a matron with children of her own. The soul who lived in the body of the aged but kindly nun is her husband in this incarnation. Because of their close ties this couple have been devoted parents but have some difficulty relating on a physical basis.

One who was Amah, or nursemaid, to a young brave on the plains of the present United States is now a child growing into manhood in that same geographical area. The former young brave is now mother to the former nursemaid.

Sagittarius

Such strange bedfellows as Japanese and Spaniards blend well into energies carried forward with this sign of the traveler. Sea-faring people both, these hardy races often set out over the ages of history to conquer foes and lands many times their size and strength. There is a daredevil quality beneath which lies a calm and calculating mind. When planets are found in this sign, the life was one of movement and separation. Perhaps a few of these natives remember a life on Noah's Ark when the ongoingness of life on this planet was seriously questioned. More likely, individuals having planets in this sign will recall more distant journeys made in spacecraft in the early ages of the globe called Terra or Earth. Planets in this sign will not be harmonious for intimate, personal relationships, but rather for the type of partnership that can withstand much diverse activity on the part of both participants. These were hot-tempered men and women who shielded their emotions behind a thin veneer of ritualistic sophistication.

A present day young man was the wife of a Phoenician sailor many hundreds of years ago in a past incarnation. She lost her former husband to his occupation. The older man who broke the news of her loved one's death is now a girl friend of the former young widow. In reversed sexual roles, the young man and woman now are working out their karma from centuries past.

Being childless is nothing new for a middle-aged couple who make their home a haven for lost cats and dogs. During a past life together in Kyoto, capital of Imperial Japan, they were separated by official duties until past the age of childbearing.

Two who shared positions on ships of the ill-fated Spanish Armada are again comrades in a shared occupational field. This lifetime both souls are in female bodies and both work as counselors to help other people through life's traumas. Many of their clients are young people who carry psychic wounds of wars.

Capricorn

The Native Americans of the eastern shore of North America, who had developed an intricate civilization long before the white man arrived, will be very special to these natives. There is an appreciation of the master organization of Mother Nature as well as the ability to move within the unaffected current. Although there is a stronger sense of personal identity, there is an understanding of the need for man to live together as the social animal which he presently is, so there is an acceptance of group order and communications.

Wherever possible, planets in this sign are happier when placed in some sort of form or sequence rather than left to random direction. Often there will be a power struggle between the two persons involved, especially if personal planets are closely conjunct. Such an attitude has occurred often in times of military stress and emphasis, such as ancient Sparta.

Although a man and woman are husband and wife during the present life, they were once sisters in the same family. During a time among the tribes known as the Cherokee, these former daughters of the same father lived together peacefully. In this lifetime the young couple share many of the same interests and can communicate freely.

A mother-in-law and daughter-in-law relationship can be difficult under the best of situations. When the present mother-in-law had once been a druid priestess who controlled the training and fate of the present daughter-in-law it calls for patience and understanding on both sides. Because the older woman is accustomed to ordering and disciplining the younger woman, she continues this trend into the present day alliance. The former druid novice automatically responds by obeying her former master, all the while resenting the intrutions into her personal life.

Aquarius
The budding scientist, the engineer, the research astrologer, the astronaut, the lonely astronomer astride his giant telescope, and many others are so close and yet so far away in time for many whose memories span the gap of time between the now and ancient Atlantean civilizations. Yet lives have intervened between as magicians in the courts of kings, as fanatics in the frontiers of new civilizations, as circus aerialists who momentarily relived the joy of soaring into space, as sea captains who set sail for distant ports, only to be carried away in search of fabled monsters, as well as dreamers whose stride through life labeled them as hobos or bums to more ambitious souls. There is little to soothe a security-ridden mate or fill the needs of ambitious partners in ties within this sign, but there is much to stir the excitement of mental probes or to enhance the search for long-lost fortunes. The miners of the California gold rush had much in common with later settlers in Alaska's northern regions. There is the same sense of loneliness, yet communion with the universe, in driving a dogsled across barren snowy wastes in the Antarctic as in piloting a spacecraft around the Moon.

So many persons who have past lives together in the sign of Aquarius remember living in the ancient land of Atlantis before man's recorded history. A present day mother and son were child and big brother in that ancient land. Two female friends were sisters and coworkers before the sinking of that island nation. An employer and her employee were mother and son in that time before history began.

Two students who are several years apart in age attend classes with the same teacher. In both cases these women have a close conjunction of planets with the present day teacher, and all three women share some pleasurable pursuits. This repeats a pattern set up centuries ago when the present teacher led this group into some innovative scientific research.

Pisces
The period around the birth and ministry of Jesus are the clearest lives for persons who have planets in Pisces. Some remember lives of Roman culture where society and soldiering held sway, while others find memories stronger of the hills around Galilee where Essenes and mystics gathered to meditate and study. Yet others are emotionally drawn by scenes of early Christians being martyred for their beliefs. For some natives, planets in this sign denote lives during which they were celibate nuns or monks in whatever religious order was dominant at the time. Although there is much compassion, there is little personal energy generated by planets in this sign between individuals. There may even be a suppression of the sexual desires when they are aroused because of the memory of past lives when personal concerns were set aside for the betterment of the entire community. The American Shakers and the Ephrata Community in Penn-

sylvania were more recent attempts to return to these concepts of life. Once this barrier has been removed, these people are kind, loving, and compassionate mates and lovers. There is always a sense of expectancy and mystery between them.

Merchants who traded their goods in either Rome or Jerusalem learned to bargain for the best terms. A mother and son in the present life, these two were storekeepers who worked and lived on the same street in pre-Christian Judea.

A young married couple in the present incarnation, a man and woman were once souls, incarnated in female bodies, who followed the teachings of the rabbi named Joshua or Jesus. The present young man was a widow and the present young woman was an unmarried maiden in the times of the Galilean.

Who Were We?

Relating with other people does not deal only with the manner in which the two or more persons behave in this particular incarnation but also the attractions or repulsions from previous lives led together. These previous patterns establish an essence or feeling between the individuals that is sometimes difficult to overcome, whether a bond of loving concern or threatening fear. Sometimes the over concern of a mother for her child becomes a stifling burden or the challenge of an adversary becomes the call to excel when these past life impressions are brought forth into a present course of action. In many cases a series of previous existences together blend and harmonize to present the couple or family with a wide choice of experiences from which to choose their present affiliations. Planets that are in conjunctions from one chart to the other indicate sojourns that have been led together and the subconscious attitudes that are imprinted upon these two souls.

When planetary energies are considered as particular people in the horoscope, it is not so much the exact individual or specific occupation that is involved, as the impression that is normally brought to mind by that type of encounter. For example, when a priestly man or woman is considered to occur in a relationship, this was merely one who greatly impressed the native concerning his or her philosophical or religious views throughout life. The identities given in this discussion are those typically accepted in our present Judeo-Christian Western culture and may differ greatly from age to age.

he primary purpose for investigating past relationships is not to return to that time period or that particular alliance, but to understand residual or subconscious emotions or sensations brought to the surface by intimacy with another individual. When delineating a comparison between two persons, it's perhaps wise not to dwell on, or even mention, such past incarnations; rather, the better choice is to inquire about unexplained impressions arising between them. In this manner, you can attempt to bring them into a discussion of sympathies such as frustration, obligation, unfounded doubts, tenderness, affection, immediate recognition of another's private desires, and competition. From such counseling can come understanding through which the couple may be released from these karmic bonds with or without realizing they are reliving past life patterns.

Other individuals always stimulate hidden qualities within each person so that the planetary energies that are triggered into activity by the presence of another being also provoke a reaction within each man, woman, or child involved. It is by turning this interrelatedness into true integration of personality that all individuals involved truly grow and develop.

The Sun in Karmic Comparisons

When considering the Sun of our solar system as a planetary force in the horoscope, it must of course remain at the center of all activity. So the principle for the Sun is the *authority figure*. This principle of power is normally considered to be exhibited by a male figure in our present and immediate past historical periods, although there may have been times of feminine domination in far distant eons when this personality was predominantly female. Whether the Sun in the horoscope is merely the father or husband, the superior at work, lord of the manor, or king in all his regal glory, the effect remains the same of being the person in charge of the lives of those who were subordinate. This energy may have been spent in a most positive and protective manner or it may have manifested in a dictatorial and cruel way. Dominion over others can be through love or fear, but it is the inevitable result of this contact. As the light of the Sun gives the warmth and energy to permit life to exist upon this planet, so the person whose Sun is conjunct a planet in another's horoscope allows that energy to be revealed within the native involved.

The Sun individual is a person, male or female, who greatly affects the formative or early years of growth and development. This may include molding and structuring the child into certain social patterns, encouraging the fruition of obvious talents and characteristics, or a tendency to dominate every action. Power can be used or misused by both persons involved just as the beach bather who remains in the bright light of the Sun over an extended period of hours, without taking the necessary precautions, is repaid with the anguish of a bad sunburn.

Often the very traits presented through the Sun in another horoscope display qualities hidden within the other native regardless of the planet with which the conjunction is formed. This represents the dislike or hatred of a weakness within the self or the pride in a less visible portion of the individual. The Sun can be either a help or a hindrance, depending on both the terms of the past associations and the present arrangements. There is always a subconscious awareness of power present between the persons involved.

Keywords are father, husband, boss, ruler, authority figure, knight, lord of the castle, master, governor, executive, guardian, employer, manager, powerful ally, and ship captain, among others having similar connotations.

Sun-Sun
Usually this relationship has existed at some period in the past as males who were equal in their rights and powers. Perhaps they were allies or enemies in a time of war or they could have coexisted as squires of friendly counties or these two persons may possibly have governed neighboring states or nations during the same time interval. There is a sense of understanding and respect even when some competition exists. Regardless of the chronological age, these individuals relate on the same level of maturity. Keywords are co-rulers, equal males, allies or foes.

Sun-Moon
As well as being the body that reflects the light of the Sun over Earth during the hours when darkness falls upon half of the globe, the Earth's Moon, or Luna, is closer to man's emotional nature, so the Moon represents the inner yearnings. As the queen is to her king, so is every woman to the man who

loves her; thus, the Moon is queen to the Sun's kingship. There are some who understand this principle as the uniting of twin souls or soul mates upon the Earth plane because of the sameness of love and understanding. However, the Sun and the Moon are not always conjunct in the horoscopes of husbands and wives, but in those who have other associations during this sojourn. Always present in the Moon person is the awareness of the true individuality of the Sun.

She, for the Moon represents a feminine principle, is there to either guide or beguile the masculine Sun entity. During the time of the relationship, the Sun person will be the aggressor and the provider for the Moon, who must become the receiver and the dependent. The Moon individual sets up the daily modes of response for both of them and determines whether the affiliation will take on the semblance of a mother-son relationship or the appearance of responsive actions between male and female. In many young people today, the Sun-Moon relationships of the past are being reversed in their present marriages, which brings about opportunities to relate in the opposite manner. Keywords are husband and wife, king and queen, lord and lady, son and doting mother, admirer and sweetheart, man and woman, or brother and sister, among others.

Sun-Mercury
Although in the times of the ancient mysteries, Mercury was considered one of the major gods who translated the edicts of heaven for mortal minds, the present interpretation of this planet tends more to deal with the period of childhood and elementary education. When the planet Mercury of one horoscope is conjunct the Sun in another natal chart, the person whose Mercury is influenced tends to endow the other entity

with a sense of glamour that may or may not be deserved. Perhaps they have lived together in a previous period when the Sun person assisted this younger man or woman to rise in his or her career endeavors. The Mercury individual tends to look to the Sun individual for counsel even though he or she sometimes resents the advice being given. In some cases, the Sun person must beware of being dictatorial to the Mercury person. Keywords are ruler and student, knight and squire, hero and admirer. star and fan, king and clown, editor and reporter, publisher and author, or principal and teacher.

Sun-Venus
The fairest maiden on Mt. Olympus could also be the vainest at times, if myths hold true. When this planet of love and desire is conjunct the Sun of another being, there will be sparks kindled between the two, for there are hidden memories of a man and woman sexually involved through love or marriage. The feminine principle of lovely Venus is as different from the connotations of the Moon as was the "bit of muslin" unlike the Victorian *hausfrau*. Rather than Venus cherishing and protecting her Sun, or king, she adores him yet expects him to court her with gifts and flattery. The Venus person may even pout if the Sun individual does not pay her enough attention, yet she will uphold his virtues in the face of criticism from others. Regardless of the present genders concerned, these individuals were once man and woman together. Keywords are master and maiden, man and mistress, king and concubine, wanderer and enchantress, giver and receiver of gifts, lord and entertainer, mandarin and geisha, buyer and lingerie salesperson, or gentleman and nail technician.

Sun-Mars

Events derived from an association with the military forces explain many of the emotions aroused between persons having a Sun and Mars conjunction between the natal horoscopes. In many cases the Mars individual readily accepts the position of working for or with the Sun person without a clear explanation of how it all came about. The Mars entity may be either protective or antagonistic toward the authoritative manner of the Sun individual, who sometimes goes as far as to desire domination at all costs. There is an unfair competition between these two persons because of previous periods when the Sun person was in a position of life-and-death jurisdiction over the Mars person. Keywords are captain and soldier, man and youth, leader and worker, dean and student, sergeant and enlistee, king and guard, trainer and slave, or guard and prisoner.

Sun-Ceres

In most cases the Sun individual loves and respects the Ceres person because of some gentleness shown during the past. There is a tie of nursing or nurturing that may have been from an older female relative or from a neighboring farmer to the young prince or nobleman. Even though this bond is strong, it does not have the lasting or sexual link of a Venus or Moon conjunction. Keywords are heir and doting mother or aunt, prince and nanny or nurse, landlord and tenant farmer, adored grandson and grandmother, lord and older maid servant, or knight and serf.

Sun-Pallas

The efficient way in which a Pallas individual carries out the directives of the Sun person explains why the natural relationship of executive and assistant or secretary feels comfortable for two natives having such a conjunction. Although other factors may lead to marriage or romance, this particular contact is one where man and woman can function as equals respecting the qualities that each brings into the association. Even though the energies suggest the existence of a male-female previous relationship, there is a platonic vibration between them. Keywords are boss and employee, chairman and secretary, diplomat and interpreter, noted author and editor or ghost writer, politician and interviewer, president and speech writer, or plantation owner and general manager.

Sun-Juno
There is a difference between having a wife who is a helpmate and one who is a shrew. This reflects the variance between the Moon and Juno, showing the legal spouse in a relationship. Beauty has often been found to be skin deep shortly after the final vows are pledged and thus it is with the wedding suggested when the Sun and Juno are conjunct in the natal horoscopes of two individuals. The Juno person seeks to be reunited with her previous mate for one of several reasons, the best of which is to reshape and resolve the past differences into a loving, caring bond. Whether the Sun is in the chart of male or female this lifetime, he will be drawn toward the Juno male or female as a bear to honey because of the past sexual attraction. At the same time the Sun person's inner instincts suggest a moment of caution and prudence, so that he approaches all interludes with the contradictory emotions of wariness and excitement. Juno can be both haughty and hurt. Keywords are husband and wife, lord and lady of the manor, man and nagging woman, provider and sponge, sire and mother of his children, suitor and frigid maiden, king and queen chosen to co-reign, members of a political alliance, or corpse and widow.

Sun-Vesta

The acolyte who aspires to imitate his bishop expresses no more hero worship than the Vesta person who contacts another's Sun by natal degree. This is why it is often difficult for these two individuals to relate on an intimate basis because a fallen idol is to be more despised than loved. Vesta represents as much the temple priestess who was physically at her priestly master's beck and call as the nun who served in a cloistered convent during later periods of history. In special cases there can be a real spiritual connection built up through teaching and sharing of religious beliefs. Keywords are chaplain and nun, pope and mother superior, pimp and prostitute, hero and worshiper, adored one and caretaker, or husband and obsessed wife.

Sun-Jupiter

By legend our present Sun Apollo pays homage to his yet powerful father and recent monarch. In truth the planet Jupiter is near the size to produce its own power source, and with its multiple Moons represents a microscopic solar system within the greater order. Astrologically, Jupiter represents a philosophical contact that expands the native's cultural understanding. These Sun-Jupiter connections may be as short-lived as a one semester student-professor classroom discussion or as lifelong as the association between an individual and the family priest. A Jupiter person may well influence and build confidence in the younger Sun person, or challenge the older Sun entity. In its best light, Jupiter is one who helps and guides with life's lessons and improvements, in the light of recognizing the true value of the Sun person. Both were usually males. Keywords are man and professor, leader and supporter, cultural and social equals, two philosophers, author and critic, host and snob, king and counselor, monarch and archbishop who crowns him, hero and proud friend, executive and confidante, or prince and advisor.

Sun-Saturn
Probably the most misunderstood energy in the solar system is that of Saturn. Even the old myths of this god as the original patron of agriculture have been forgotten in lieu of the concepts of karma, troubles, and suppression. Without Saturn there would be no form, no skin, and no support system to sustain life on this planet. The strongest impression that comes through in Sun and Saturn conjunctions is that of thorough teaching of the young prince being prepared for his rightful position of power. Saturn will show the Sun his faults and urge him to take advantage of opportunities to change. Nevertheless, it is to Saturn that the Sun person turns in time of distress to receive comfort and permanent security. Keywords are prince and tutor, man and father, student and teacher, general and commander of permanent base, hero and jealous older person, criminal and jailer, lord of the castle and leader of the siege forces, ship captain and owner of the line, husband and father-in-law, or president of company and chairman of the board.

Sun-Uranus
As the planetary energy that most suggests the entire field of scientific research and development, Uranus also brought back to man's consciousness some of the reminders of the lost (or fabled) continent of Atlantis. These times and types of individuals are often brought to mind when planets conjunct Uranus from one horoscope to another. In more recent periods of history Uranus persons seem to have served Sun individuals as court astrologers and magicians, as clever men of futuristic thought, and as lawless rebels. Because of the

slow movement of Uranus through the skies, there will be many such alliances during a lifetime. A five-degree orb will allow this conjunction between all persons born during a two to three year interval having the Sun in the present Uranus sign. Thus, the Sun-Uranus contact is more generational than personal. Keywords are ruler and court astrologer, commander and test pilot, king and anarchist, executive and genius, lord of the manor and rebel, or master and lawless one.

Sun-Neptune

Because the planet Neptune remains in each tropical zodiac sign approximately fourteen years, any conjunctions found between the Sun and Neptune will represent that the Neptune individual was merely one of a body of persons living or working under the reign of this particular king or Sun ruler. There is usually not a personal relationship suggested by this particular connection. Neptune could have been one of a number of monks or priests who served the temples during the reign of the Sun. In other time periods Neptune would have been a healer, musician or poet to soothe and entertain the harried executive. Keywords are king and priest, ruler and religious advisor, lord of the manor and nun or monk, knight and wandering minstrel, man and healer or physician, querent and medium, patient and prayer leader, captain and sage, or guardian and liar.

Sun-Pluto

The length and variation with which Pluto is found in the various zodiacal signs suggests that it represents the cultural changes the entire world was undergoing during any specific period rather than personal relationships or alliances. During a time of sexual freedom, a Pluto-Sun conjunction meant the release of more physical energy than during a more Puritanical age when zeal flowed toward conducting purges and chastising. With a Sun- Pluto conjunction there is often a clash of strong wills, sometimes between persons of differing ages, or the Sun person will have a personal Sun-Pluto conjunction in his or her own horoscope. Keywords are prince and dictator, ruler and assassin, man and childhood nightmares, executive and his psychologist, or captain and mutineer.

Considering the Moon in Karmic Comparisons

The Moon is the body that reflects the light of the Sun for beings living on Earth. It also determines the tides of the mighty oceans and helps to keep Earth's atmospheric pressures balanced. Without the physical Moon, Earth would not be habitable for the species found on it today. Other planets have their moon or moons handling different variables for their planetary conditions. The title properly given for our moon is Luna. This is the term from which the word lunatic was derived, for the Moon is known to affect emotional stability.

The Moon represents the primary feminine principle in astrology, for it stands for the mother who reproduces and cares for the young of the race. Although this is one of the primary functions of all females, the care and nurture of young are also a part of every male entity.

The Moon deals with thought forms from the past and with the subconscious mind, rather than ongoing interests. There is a sort of automatic response, or need, expressed with the Moon, rather than the logical analysis of the Sun. Sometimes the word "mother" is used interchangeably with the term "moon," and this can be considered either as mothering or smothering. Keywords are mother, wife, medium, cook, sailor, receptive person, female, opinionated individual, domestic, family interests, martyr, and woman.

Moon-Moon
The most common relationship found when the two individuals have their Moons conjunct is persons who were reared in the same family environment. These women may have been sisters, cousins reared by the same set of parents, wives of the same husband living in a common harem, concubines of the same master, or two girls assigned to the same orphanage. Whatever their background, it will be similar. And the mother figure for each will be alike. Keywords are co-wives, sisters, like females, harem dwellers, cousins.

Moon-Mercury
The Moon individual tends to smother the Mercury person even as she is being soothing and kind. However, the ever-active Mercury individual keeps the Moon on her toes and takes time to talk things out and to keep open the door to communication. In some cases the Moon person has been a nurse or caretaker for an emotionally disturbed child. In other instances the Mercury person has been the interpreter for an emotionally crushed woman. These may be women of different ages who enjoy each other's company. Keywords are mother and child, cook and maid, restaurant owner and server, lady and squire, two friends of different ages.

Moon-Venus
There may be some competition or jealousy between these two women from the past because the mother image is not always glad to lose a husband or lover to a raving young

beauty. In other cases these two past life females may be the best of friends. The Venus person lacks sympathy for the Moon individual. Keywords are sister and sister, mother and beautiful daughter, wife and mistress, woman and dance instructor, matron and beautician, spouse and sister-in-law, female and photographer, friendly women.

Moon-Mars

With so much physical and emotional energy generated between two individuals, there are bound to be either strong positive or negative feelings. A person will often react to a person having Mars conjunct her Moon out of past fears and jealousies. There will be resentment if the Moon individual tries to possess the Mars person or threaten his freedom in any way. During past incarnations these two individuals have been torn apart because of the impulsive actions of the Mars male personality. In the past the Moon would have been a female entity and the Mars a male. Keywords are mother and soldier son, woman and flirtatious man, doting mama and rebellious son, possessive woman and male relative, female and carpenter, queen and her guardsman, or maiden and abductor.

Moon-Ceres

Disagreement on details may be common between two women having a Moon and Ceres conjunction between their natal horoscopes. One is the mother principle and the other is the objective nurturing concept; thus the Moon may have been the biological mother whose child was reared by the Ceres nanny or nurse. The emotional outbursts of the Moon are not looked upon favorably by the Ceres person. Keywords are mother and nursemaid, woman and nurse, wife and servant, housekeeper and produce farmer, female and stepmother, princess and godmother, orphan girl and foster mother.

Moon-Pallas

Usually the Moon individual appreciates the competent Pallas person but does not really wish to be around her much of the time. These two persons are quite different by temperament and will have difficulty with the daily details of living together. The Moon person wants to live at a leisurely rate and enjoy sensations around her, while the Pallas individual prefers to direct the activity in her environment. Keywords are mother and career woman, wife and husband's assistant, older female and young office worker, woman and accountant, or aunt and niece.

Moon-Juno

If the past association occurred between women of very different ages, there will be pleasant memories for these two entities. However, this can be the conjunction of planets showing jealousy over a man in a past life. The Moon woman of the past and the Juno female of the past have been in love with, or married to, the same husband. These two individuals usually want the same things out of life but are not anxious to share with each other. Keywords are mother and lovely daughter, woman and lady of the manor, older queen and lady in waiting, woman and her seamstress, mother-in-law and insecure wife, or woman and her social superior.

Moon-Vesta

The individual with the Moon conjunct Vesta in another's horoscope usually reveres the Vesta individual. In a past association this could have been a proud mother who saw her beloved daughter enter the life of a celibate nun or dedicate her days to the service of humanity. In several cases this contact showed years of nursing and care for a delicate child by the Moon mother. The Vesta person usually responds with gratitude and appreciation, although she will be embarrassed by public affection. Keywords are mother and nun, bereaved wife and priestess at the temple, old woman and unmarried daughter, abandoned woman and her social worker, loving mama and delicate daughter, or two religious women.

Moon-Jupiter
Any mother having such an intelligent and beautiful son will tend to spoil him in this or any other life time. In a past association this conjunction shows a Moon mother who made things exceptionally easy for the person who is represented by the Jupiter. There is a thread of overpro- tectiveness going both ways with this conjunction. Keywords are mother and son who became a priest, mother and philosopher offspring, widowed mother and adored only son, female and wealthy friend or benefactor, matriarch and her counselor, or queen and her social equal.

Moon-Saturn
Even though there is a tendency for the Saturn person to expect excellent results from the Moon individual's activity, there is also a protective quality between these two entities. During a past incarnation the Moon may have been the elder daughter of the Saturn man or the mother of a scholarly son. The Moon female sometimes spends years caring for the aging father represented by Saturn. There is an automatic response for the Moon female to look to Saturn for approval. Keywords are woman and elderly father, female and banker, maiden and guardian, woman and jailer, mother and scholarly son, widow and eldest child, or female student and professor.

Moon-Uranus
This is not as personal a contact as some others, but the Uranus person will bring excitement and changes into the Moon individual's life. There is no understanding of the daily living patterns of each other, so quarrels are commonplace. In some cases the Uranus entity has been a teacher or a leader for the Moon in past times. Keywords are woman and innovative teacher, female and astrologer, queen and court advisor, mother and engineering son, maiden and rebel leader, or woman and scientist.

Moon-Neptune
There can be either deception or great spiritual rapport between these two persons. In past lives the Neptune person may have been a priest who comforted and inspired the Moon. However, the opposite has been found true in several cases when the Neptune entity deceived the Moon person in the past life. Keywords are queen and teacher of religion, woman and chaplain, female and deceiving lover, wife and thief, lovely maiden and romantic serenader, female and sailor, or woman and priestly brother.

Moon-Pluto
In more than one way this conjunction of planets can be sexually exciting and emotionally devastating. During past incarnations these individuals may have had an intense encounter, but not a lasting relationship. The excitement generated between them is not sufficient devotion upon which to build a lasting association unless other factors are present in their horoscopes. Keywords are queen and assassin, female and dictator, mother and gangster son, woman and kidnapper, maid and her guru, or gypsy wife and lover.

Considering Mercury in Karmic Comparisons

If one statement had to be made about the essence of Mercury, it would be "interest in giving a name to every being, thing, and emotion in existence." There is an abiding occupation with languages and cultures. Mercury wants to learn to express symbolic intentions in literal words. This planet emits the vibrations of either a young man or a young woman because it is neuter by gender. The Mercury influenced individual learns through personal study, while the Jupiter person learns through experience. This is why Mercury is thought of as the perpetual student. The expression may not be that of a young person but only of an entity with an open and inquiring mind. When this planet is conjunct a planet of another person in the natal horoscope comparisons, Mercury represents the one who has been taught or supported by the other person.

Mercury represents a brother or sister of another person, simply meaning that they grew up together in the same environmental structure. There is an understanding where Mercury is concerned and the ability to talk with each other.

Keywords are art or drama critic, linguist, student, script writer, traveler, signer for the deaf, reader for the blind, messenger, author, orator, scribe, squire, thinker, reporter, sibling, radio commentator, telephone or telegraph operator, or guide.

Mercury-Mercury
There is a feeling of having lived before in the same location, whether it is a home, village, or orphanage. With this combination of planets, both individuals will be able to freely ex-

press their ideas and feelings with each other. Often there is no emotional closeness, but rather the awareness of having been interested in studying the same subject both in the past and now in the present. In some cases these two persons lack the same one of the five senses, such as being deaf or blind. Keywords are children of the same parents, having lived in the same home, students in the same classroom, friends who talked together, or reporters for the same news outlet.

Mercury-Venus

The Mercury individual has learned to appreciate beauty and art through an earlier association with this Venus person. During their past incarnation(s) together there was a sharing of the finer things that wealth and influence can bring. The Venus person expects the Mercury entity to continue to learn and develop each time they are together. Venus usually represents a female figure of the past, while Mercury may have been either a young man or another woman during their past association. Mercury will be prone to continue a habit begun during past lives—that of bringing Venus valuable gifts that bring a smile to her lips. Keywords are child and big sister, critic and artist or musician, teenager and beautician, youth and beauty queen, script writer and renowned actress, or friends.

Mercury-Mars

A streak of selfishness is aroused in the Mercury person by association with an individual having Mars conjunct her or his Mercury. Sometimes this alliance brings out the negative egotism in both parties. Mars does stimulate and excite the Mercury mind with ideas, and they are good opponents in a debating match. These two entities will be quite rowdy together as they may once have been brothers engaged in disorderly conduct. Mars brings out more of the masculine side of the Mercury person. During past incarnations, Mercury has been the cadet to Mars' upperclass status in a military academy, or the two may even have shared a boxing ring together. Keywords are youth and petty criminal, file clerk and police officer, sibling and big brother, teacher and boisterous student, recruit and soldier, boxers or debaters.

Mercury-Ceres

The child who looked up to her nursemaid or Amah had almost the attitude of obedience and respect as had the young nun for the hospital administrator. In the not too distant past on the American plains, the traveler or soldier looked to his Native American guide for advice and assurance. This combination of planets between people gives the Mercury person a sense of security and forces the Ceres individual to accept an attitude of responsible action. Ceres must set examples for the Mercury person regardless of their present differences, even when there is a great age span. Keywords are child and nanny, file clerk and nurse, volunteer and hospital administrator, traveler and guide, squire and housemaid, telephone operator and farm wife.

Mercury-Pallas

Pallas always supports and prompts the Mercury person to grow and expand his or her abilities. This shows past associations of the Pallas person being an instructor/teacher for the Mercury individual. Although Mercury is normally considered the teacher for the young child, Pallas is the instructor for the partially trained person, while Jupiter is the college professor for the experiences in life that give wisdom. Mercury has been a young lady of quality who was taught needlepoint and fine stitchery by an older woman who was the

48

Pallas individual in a past incarnation. Or Mercury could have been a young squire who was taught the fine points of horsemanship by an older stable hand now incarnated as the entity having Pallas conjunct his Mercury. Relationships were usually platonic. Keywords are student and instructor, handicraft worker and instructor, media employee and female politician, student and riding instructor, messenger and executive assistant.

Mercury-Juno
The Mercury person always lightens and makes life more cheerful for the prim and proper Juno person. This may have been in the guise of a young lady-in-waiting for the dame of the manor in Medieval Days or as the charming flower girl for the wealthy bride. The Juno person insists that the Mercury individual observe all the rules and restrictions forced by society upon their relationship, but privately rejoices in Mercury's little escapades. Keywords are flower girl and bride, writer and matron, reporter and society leader, companion and lady, or speaker and patroness.

Mercury-Vesta
The Mercury person will adapt to and for the Vesta individual in the present incarnation as she or he did in their past lives together. There is a sense of awe from Mercury toward the dedicated Vesta as the orphan for the generous nun who cared for her during a dreary childhood. Some cases are known where Mercury was a messenger or liaison between the priests of the temple and the vestal virgins serving the same god. In this manner the young child became associated with the lovely maiden whose Vesta is now conjunct his Mercury. Even when Mercury was male and Vesta was a female by gender, theirs was not a sexual relationship but one

of mental understanding. Keywords are child and nun, signer and deaf person, novice and mother superior, neophyte and temple server, or girl and older sister.

Mercury-Jupiter

Even though Mercury is the teacher, he or she has much to learn from Jupiter as the college professor. In many past incarnations Mercury has been found to be a lifelong student of the Jupiter person. The Jupiter individual led the Mercury entity through various experiences to help them both learn and evolve together. In many cases during the Middle Ages in Europe, the Jupiter entity lived in the body of a male priest of the church, for that was where learning and culture were centered during that time period. Keywords are child and minister, student and professor, critic and publisher, linguist and traveler, squire and king's counselor, orator and promoter, client and lawyer, or reporter and editor.

Mercury-Saturn

There is a demand to organize the life—or else—from the Saturn individual to the Mercury person. Saturn insists that Mercury fulfill his or her responsibilities. There is a push for discipline and order in their relationship. Mercury develops wisdom from this association; however, he or she often feels restricted. In the past the Saturn person was an authority figure such as an aged parent for the Mercury individual. There is no one else who gives Mercury the sense of material security that Saturn does. This is the person to whom the Mercury entity has turned to life after life for financial backing and encouragement. Even when Saturn has served as his or her jailer, the Mercury person has felt protected. Keywords are truant and jailer, student and principal or disciplinarian, adult and aged parent, file clerk and employer, or reporter and governor.

Mercury-Uranus
Uranus makes the Mercury person emotional and excitable as well as bringing interests into his or her life. These two individuals enhance the awareness latent within each other. They can both be quite opinionated. During past lives the Uranus person helped the Mercury individual escape what seemed a dull and dreary existence. Mercury found there was excitement but lack of security with Uranus. Both of these entities have lived in either male or female bodies during their past lives together. Keywords are novice and fanatic, recruit and proselytizer, student and rebel teacher, or reporter and dictator.

Mercury-Neptune
Neptune either inspires or deceives the Mercury person. When two persons have Neptune and Mercury conjunct, they have great extrasensory perception together or both are escape artists. Neptune teaches Mercury his tricks either way. The chances of both being males in past incarnations are stronger than not. In some cases Neptune was the village priest or spiritual adviser for the inquiring young student. Keywords are typist and poet, squire and chaplain, child and photographer, student and visiting magician, client and medium, or penitent parishioner and priest.

Mercury-Pluto
The college student has always been attracted to the rebel leader or fanatical speaker. Whether he or she follows this individual to fame or ruin depends on other factors in the horoscope. A connection between Pluto and Mercury between charts shows this attraction of mind and emotions. Keywords are recruit and rebel leader, student and occultist, youth and speaker on reincarnation, or reporter and political reformer.

Considering Venus in Karmic Comparisons

The key to understanding Venus is to truly comprehend the concept of material possessions. One of the greatest attributes a human being has is the ability to show love for both self and another person. This is the principle of perfected manifestation. It is impossible to actually love another individual without first understanding and loving one's self. To achieve this goal, one must come to an awareness of who and what he is under the veneer of public behavior. It means getting to know the soul or spirit behind the physical body and the emotional personality. These inner states are revealed through contacts with other people. Each person reflects certain attributes of those in his or her immediate surroundings.

Behind the emotional desires of Venus is the need for fulfillment in union with another. This yearning for conscious harmony is a basic part of the human race. Venus is the ability to draw others into one's intimate circle. It can extract the benefits from any association or alliance. When used in the purest manner, Venus can reach the highest expression of man's essential nature. This is why the planet is associated with song and dance, with artistry and poetry. Venus represents man's aesthetic and social urges, which lead toward mutual development.

On the other hand, a negatively expressed Venus can be jealous and selfish. A woman scorned can pout and berate her closest friends. Venus represents the appetites and desires that can be used solely on the sexual plane or that can be elevated to a spiritual sharing. Overindulgence over a period of incarnations may be difficult to overcome during any one lifetime. Keywords are artist, singer, dancer, party giver, joyous female, acknowledged beauty, young woman, sympathizer, cosmetologist, nail technician, model, fashion-plate, dieter, mistress, or indolent woman.

Venus-Venus

When the two Venus planets are conjunct in the natal horoscope comparison between two people, there will be shared interests. The way they enjoy life will be similar and they will choose the same type of recreation. If there are no other conjunctions, there may not be enough stimulation and variety for the relationship to last very long. There are so many things to agree about that it is not worth arguing about minor details. In past incarnations these two persons will have shared female pursuits together whether shopping for interesting clothing or planning menus. They may have been members of the same ballet troupe or shared the program as debutantes during the same season. Keywords are sisters, women friends, members of the same ballet troupe, choir members, performers of piano duets, partners in a beauty shop or venture, or jewelers.

Venus-Mars

There is no doubt with this combination that these individuals were lovers in a past life. The Venus female personality adored the male Mars entity with all his violence and possessiveness. If the sexual roles are reversed for the present incarnation, there will be a tendency to relate as in the past with Mars being the more aggressive of the two. Such a pairing shows a definite past association as a strong physical tie and leaves the door open for a lifetime of sharing. Venus brings to the Mars individual a desire for love and refinement through the union. And Mars polarizes the assertiveness of the relationship. Keywords are lovers, wife and husband, mother and father of a family, mistress and lover, woman and man, or lady and her knight.

Venus-Ceres
The Ceres individual will be protective and slightly disapproving of the Venus person in this association. Since both entities were female figures during the past life together there will be more of a mother and daughter relationship than a physical tie. In many instances the Ceres individual was the nursemaid, or Amah, for the spoiled young lady whose Venus is now conjunct her Ceres. Keywords are wife and farmer, lady and nanny, girl and stepmother, daughter and mother, orphan and custodian, patient and nurse, or mistress and housemaid.

Venus- Pallas
There is not a strong personal tie between this pair of planets in conjunction between charts. The Venus personality is not too inclined to enjoy studying and training periods, whereas Pallas likes nothing better than to discipline and instruct the fledgling artist. In some instances, Pallas was found to be an expert craftsman living during the times when the Venus person desired fine jewelry or furnishings. Keywords are shopper and silversmith, artist and supplier of paints, mistress and skilled female worker, model and instructor, or housewife and interior decorator.

Venus-Juno
These two persons understand each other's basic desires and may sometimes come to an impasse over who is to get her own way. In the past, these souls would have been in female forms and may have been in competition for love of the same man. When this is true, the Juno individual would have been

54

the legal wife, while Venus had his love and affection. Even with the jealousy between these individuals there is sympathy of each other's position in life. Keywords are mistress and wife, competitors, woman and dressmaker, ballerina and patroness of the arts, or professional mourner and weeping widow.

Venus-Vesta

For this combination there is little understanding of the motivation behind each other's actions. The Venus person cannot really comprehend devoting one's self to a course of action where personal desires must be put aside. And Vesta in turn considers Venus to be rather selfish and indulgent. Many times the Vesta person was a nun or member of a strict religious sect while Venus was a young lady of society who had little thought for those less fortunate. Keywords are laywoman and nun, matron and temple priestess.

Venus-Jupiter

Between these two happy and gregarious people there will be a lot of joy. They may indulge each other with rich foods and expensive gifts to the pleasure of both. Sometimes a fat and happy wife is better than a skinny, unhappy one. Venus related in the past to this Jupiter as a lovely female who enticed him with her charms. Jupiter in turn was an older, more sophisticated man who may have held a title or a government position. Whether they sanctified their love with a legal marriage is immaterial. There is an immediate responsiveness between these two people. Keywords are flirt and government official, woman and man, beauty queen and professor, divorced woman and lawyer, or mistress and lover.

Venus-Saturn

Joy is sacrificed to responsibility in this relationship. Here love is dominated by thoughts of duty. The ability to fulfill emotional desires may be thwarted by ignorance or fear. Certainly where these two planets are conjunct there is a constancy and fidelity on the part of both companions. Venus has been a beautiful young woman who relied on the security and wisdom of the masculine Saturn in a past life. In some cases this protectiveness of Saturn became stifling for the Venus person. Keywords are lovely lady and strict teacher, woman and aged father, dancer and choreographer, romanticist and realist, or wife and older husband.

Venus-Uranus

This relationship can bring supreme joy or terrible anguish. There will certainly not be boredom between people having this combination of planets. The Uranus person brings excitement into the daily routine of the Venus individual. In the past Venus may have been a woman who eloped with such an exciting young man as Uranus was. This can be invigorating but also nerve-racking. When this relationship is analyzed it falls apart, for it is based on pure emotion. Keywords are lady and mad scientist, mistress and passionate lover, female and political radical, singer and eccentric musician, or wife and abductor.

Venus-Neptune

Neptune has a response to the beauty of the Venus person, and reacts by creating an illusion to entrap the Venus entity. The particular fashion or vogue of the moment may wear thin for the Venus person as soon as she realizes what she has given up for this dream. In the past Neptune either inspired or deceived the woman who was Venus. She could have been his beautiful assistant in a traveling magic act Keywords are woman and priest, disciple and master, female assistant and magician, famous beauty and poet, or wife and unfaithful husband.

Venus-Pluto

For a person having this combination with her natal Venus, the personal Pluto will also be in conjunction. Pluto is a generational planet and has little personal effect. These two individuals live in a time when the culture is exerting pressure on the Venus person to change his or her ideas of love and beauty. This merely doubles the demand for Venus to face the reality of the present situation. In the past these entities have been associated with groups which were promoting major changes in government or society. Keywords are dieter and resort manager, renown beauty and plastic surgeon, model and fashion designer, or investor and banker.

Considering Mars in Karmic Comparisons

The image that comes most often to mind with mention of Mars is the mighty warrior of the past or the prominent sports figure of today. This view of the masculine personality is still common even with the present trend toward a blending of the male and female halves of each individual.

Another way of looking at Mars energy is to consider it an awareness of the individual. Whereas Venus wants to be drawn to other people, Mars wishes to push people away. This is the emotion that disrupts relationships rather than binds them closer together. The Mars part of each person is concerned with protecting his or her individuality. From this frame of reference he sees everyone else as an enemy or an obstacle to his personal freedom and success.

Fulfillment for the Mars element is freedom and productive employment. This is why it is so important to blend the female and male portions of each person. When a person is too feminine, he or she is too passive to protect himself or herself or to accomplish anything. When a person allows the masculine energies to hold sway, he or she has difficulty getting along with other people even in group situations.

During past lives the planet Mars represents incarnations when the soul was living in a masculine body and acting out an aggressive role. Other lives in a male body may have been more subtle and less energetic.

Keywords are young man, soldier, sports figure, surgeon, gladiator, dentist, carpenter, warrior, swordsman, militia, worker, machinist, train engineer, primitive tribesman, Native American brave, hunter, guard, petty criminal, laborer, courageous youth, or barber.

Mars-Mars
Two people with Mars conjunct will seem to be locked in combat a great deal of the time. This is fine if they are soldiers in training or members of the same football team, but difficult in a marriage or family grouping. In the past these two individuals were involved in an aggressive and impulsive way. They may have been competitors or have lived as tribal brothers. Certainly that past life would have seen both souls clothed with a masculine body. Keywords are mortal enemies, soldier and soldier, Native American brave and warrior, machinist and worker, fencer and swordsman, or two wrestlers.

Mars-Ceres

Ceres takes the initiative in trying to tame and domesticate the Mars individual, which immediately creates strife. However, there is the remembrance of the tender care from Ceres when the Mars person was a little boy, so he tries not to hurt her feelings or be too gruff. The Mars person feels babied and confined when around the Ceres entity, no matter what their present relationship. Their earlier association was probably as young boy and his nursemaid. In a marriage this can create sexual problems if the past life memories are strong. Ceres wants to plan the day's activities and exercises just as she did in the past for the young Mars individual. This protective attitude will be resented in a close association in the present Keywords are boy and nursemaid, warrior and healer, carpenter and housemaid, surgeon and nurse, brave and herb lady, or hunter and woman who dressed the hides.

Mars-Pallas

While Pallas appreciates the industry of the Mars individual, she still wants to instruct him in proper procedures. If Mars is a diligent and humble worker, so much the better for the Pallas, who can be a kind and helpful teacher. However, if Mars rebels at this state of affairs, there will be war for sure between these two individuals. In a past life these two were a military figure of some sort and an instructor or trainer. Mars would have been in the male body, and Pallas may have been either male or female. Keywords are swordsman and fencing instructor, criminal and social worker, gladiator and trainer, or knight and horse trainer.

Mars-Juno

In this relationship each one is afraid the other will get the best of the situation or win one more argument. These people do not trust each other completely. Between these two individuals there is a strong physical magnetism, but a barrier to freely showing loving affection. During a past incarnation, they may have been soldier husband and wife, or they may only have been lovers. Juno tends to restrict Mars' sense of freedom. Mars feels that Juno's demands are unreasonable and her expectations beyond his ability to fulfill them. Juno feels socially superior. Keywords are husband and wife, soldier and lady of the manor, guard and queen, rapist and female victim, petty criminal and wealthy homeowner. murderer and widow of victim, or explorer and vigilant wife.

Mars-Vesta
Mars often rejects the restrictiveness of Vesta when they are thrown together for any reason. There is a lack of understanding between them of each other's respective motives. Mars can respect Vesta's allegiance to a cause, for any soldier must believe in the cause for which he or she fights; but he or she cannot comprehend the limitations put on free-time activities. During a past life these two souls were not closely related but had a rather distant association. Vesta, as a healing woman or nursing nun, has cared for the wounded male who now has Mars conjunct her Vesta. Keywords are brave and medicine woman, active young man and meditator, crusader and religious celibate, soldier and pacifist, or extrovert and introvert.

Mars-Jupiter
The Jupiter person appeals to Mars' sense of honor and courage, and gets him to do all sorts of work simply for approval. These two individuals were probably associated during the Age of Chivalry as gentleman and warrior. They are cheerful and easygoing in each other's company. There is a friendly

impersonality between them. This association can be supportive in a business sense, but add little to a personal relationship. Keywords are soldier and philosopher, young man and older playboy, carpenter and architect. bus driver and traveler, waiter and gourmet, guard and wealthy homeowner, or sports professional and financial backer.

Mars-Saturn

Mars feels restrained by an emotional bondage in this relationship with Saturn. This can be painful for both persons. Saturn makes the Mars individual feel inferior or deficient without meaning to exert this influence. There may be an age difference between these two people in this incarnation. Saturn, as the former father, tries to hold Mars back from impulsive and dangerous actions. This attempt to restrain Mars' aggressiveness is taken as an effort to emasculate him. There is no way for Saturn to reason with the Mars person because their avenues of communication are missing. In the past life, Saturn was an older and stern father figure to the impulsive young Mars. Keywords are son and father, warrior and chieftain, criminal and jailer, boy and disciplinarian, or titled gentleman and heir.

Mars-Uranus

This relationship makes both people feel like free souls. Although they may be passionate and intense in their activities together, the Mars and Uranus individuals have not related on an intimate basis before. Because of the slow motion of Uranus, there will be many persons who have this conjunction for the Mars individual. This combination of planets can bring out rebel tendencies in the already volatile Mars person. Keywords are soldier and rebel, campaigner and politician, machinist and engineer, hunter and ecologist, laborer and scientist, or youth and libertine.

Mars-Neptune

There is a sense of frustration between these two people because of the lack of understanding. Constant contact with the Neptune individual can cause deep neuroses in the Mars person. Of course, with this conjunction, the Mars entity would also have a conjunction with his or her own natal Neptune, so the picture is never clear in the comparison. Neptune won't give Mars the clear-cut answers he or she wants to hear. Keywords are surgeon and pharmacist, warrior and dreamer, tribesman and witch doctor, sports figure and ballet dancer, or lover and celibate monk.

Mars-Pluto

The generational changes represented by Pluto excite and impel the Mars individual. This combination, as well as his or her own personal Pluto conjunction, adds to the need for personal freedom. These two can be helpful to each other in implementing a rapid turnover of ideas and activities. Keywords are police officer and detective, laborer and oil refiner, miner and mine operator, or warrior and war chief.

Considering Jupiter in Karmic Comparisons

The primary moving force behind Jupiter's actions is that of assisting others. He wants to constantly expand and improve the environment and those within it. Jupiter is ever concerned with the principle of social justice as shown by his role as a lawyer or judge. He loves to guide the younger, undeveloped people around him in order to assist them to unfold spiritually, emotionally and materially. Jupiter attempts to bring spiritual concepts into a usable form and thus invigorate and uplift the entire race of humanity.

In many cases Jupiter incarnates as the concerned counselor or clergy person. He must in these cases beware of developing false pride in his own benevolent acts. Because of the bounty surrounding the Jupiter individual, he can bring out the emotions of extravagance and greed in associates. This entity is usually pictured as a successful man in the very prime of life.

Because of the desire to give, Jupiter often spoils loved ones. When Jupiter is rebuffed or thwarted, he retreats behind a compensation complex. At this stage the Jupiter person attempts to buy love and affection through the giving of lavish gifts because of the need to be appreciated.

When the full splendor and pageantry associated with positive Jupiter's action are played out, there is a completion of the full circle of giving and receiving. Only when gratitude is genuinely expressed by the receiver is the circle of giving completed. With love a gift is purchased or made and presented, and with full appreciation and love should it be received. When there are doubts or apprehension on the part of either party, the spiral of love is not completed and cannot move forward.

Just as Mercury teaches through use of the spoken and written word, Pallas instructs through example and repetition of proper procedures, so Jupiter teaches through exposing the student to experiences of life. Thus the best gifts from Jupiter contain a mixture of blessings and evil so they may provide varying fortunes. Keywords are minister, physician, lawyer, philanthropist, prophet, guru, professor, traveler, sportsman, horseback rider, editor, publisher, friend of the family, patron of the arts, or social elitist.

Jupiter-Jupiter

These two individuals share the same optimistic view of the world. They may travel around the globe together or merely enjoy fine cooking in the best restaurants. The desire for harmony assists this in being a peaceful, yet possibly dull, relationship. Keywords are rector and rabbi, fellow travelers, patron of the symphony and backer of the ballet, host and happy guest, editor and publisher, director and producer, or prophet and guru.

Jupiter-Ceres

Jupiter is more easygoing than Ceres and certainly more prone to spend large amounts of money. When Jupiter was the doting father of her young charge in a past incarnation, the Ceres nanny disapproved of the father's ways in spoiling the child. These two persons will not have the same innate life style or way of spending leisure time. Keywords are wealthy man and maidservant, joyful father and nanny, physician and nurse, or honored professor and farm woman.

Jupiter-Pallas

Pallas tends to interpret the actions of Jupiter in a positive way, while Jupiter will compliment Pallas for a job well done. These two may have been benevolent father and daughter in a past life. Often Jupiter, as a male, has been like a godfather or wealthy uncle to the young Pallas female. Keywords are proud father and professional daughter, art patron and talented weaver, member of the hunt and horse trainer, professor and assistant, traveler and interpreter or companion, or minister and assistant.

Jupiter-Juno

Both of these persons are very aware of their social status. They enjoy large-scale entertaining, especially if the guest list is complete with important personages. Juno would like for Jupiter to pay her more personal attention, but she is satisfied with the glamour that Jupiter brings into her life. These two have probably been husband and wife in a past incarnation. Lineage is important to both of these individuals. Keywords are financier and treasurer of the board, husband and wife, philanthropist and patroness of the arts, king and queen, or benefactor and mistress.

Jupiter-Vesta
Because Vesta tries to restrain Jupiter's expansiveness, she bothers him. This female wants Jupiter to be more concerned with keeping the status quo. In extreme cases, Jupiter was Vesta's guru even when he did not want to be placed in such a deified position. During a past life they have been a pope and a lowly nun, or a lama and a temple servant There is not much upon which to build a personal relationship between these two planets. Keywords are chaplain and nun, minister and Altar Guild volunteer, or guru and disciple.

Jupiter-Saturn
While Jupiter prefers companionship, Saturn would rather live in isolation. There is a power struggle between these two persons because both wish to be in the driver's seat at all times. Jupiter feels choked up by Saturn's fixed attitudes toward everything. Reputation is important to each of these persons for very different reasons. They could build a good check-and-balance system if they would pull together in team fashion. In the past life together, these two were men who held varying political and religious views and opposed each other. Keywords are social leader and puritan, spendthrift and miser, rabbi and president of the congregation, rector and bishop, or company president and chairman of the board.

Jupiter-Uranus

This combination is like harnessing a young nobleman with a union organizer. Their great expectations will soon turn to disappointment in this relationship. There is a constant fluctuation of ideas and activity because there is not a solid foundation of understanding upon which to build. Keywords are absent-minded professor and scientist, prince and union organizer, politician and rebel, or conservative publisher and scandal sheet editor.

Jupiter-Neptune

These two can be each other's guardian angels or escape valves. They have worked together in the past in hospitals or orphanages. However, a life of delusion would have been just as possible. Jupiter, as a minister or clergyman, and Neptune, as an open-minded physician, form an excellent healing team. Keywords are minister and chaplain, an optimist and a pessimist, director and actor, patron and musician, physician and healer, or gentleman and troubadour.

Jupiter-Pluto

Both of these individuals like to see changes take place. Jupiter would prefer to watch the natural course of events flow past his window, whereas Pluto wants to be part of the action. Since Pluto moves so slowly, it brings more generational changes and would influence the culture in which the Jupiter individual lives rather than the personal relationship. Keywords are lawyer and lobbyist, clergyman and social worker, philosopher and psychiatrist, or traveler and immigration official.

Considering Saturn in Karmic Comparisons

Saturn's primary focus is to oversee each situation with the aim of forcing every individual involved to achieve as much as he or she is capable of doing. Fulfillment of purpose and complete use of talents is significant to the Saturn leader. People feel that Saturn is blighting or suppressing, when he is only demanding that responsibilities be carried out. Saturn brings people back to earth from their dream worlds.

Often the presence of Saturn in a comparison conjunction brings out the other person's need for emotional or material security in associations. The father aspect of Saturn conveys whether materials or talents have been rightly or wrongly used. The other individual finds himself or herself virtually reporting every action to the Saturn contact in order to receive approval or scolding.

A strong sense of form and security emanates from the Saturn entity toward others in his or her close vicinity. In some cases a Saturn tie has been from a retarded child or crippled adult who relied on another for complete support and care. In either case, a strong dependency held the relationship together regardless of petty quarrels and resentments. This combination of love-hates remains in the present alliance.

When dealing closely with Saturn, it becomes necessary to distinguish between duty and responsibility. It is necessary to determine the difference between duties that are imposed upon the individual by society or by an employer and the true responsibility to promote the growth and evolution of the soul during this sojourn in the Earth plane; the two are quite distinct.

When there is a reaction of fear from an individual toward a Saturn contact, this comes of the former person's own sense of self-inadequacy or his or her dread of facing possible failure. An honest evaluation of personal qualifications followed by the effort to succeed always gains approval of a Saturn associate. All this practical planet requires is constructive attitude and activity.

Keywords are older person, rigid or responsible man, patriarch, governor, principal, employer, statesman, shepherd, conservative, father, disciplinarian, chairman of the board, grandfather, Father Time, jailer, owner, eldest son, or realist.

Saturn-Saturn
These individuals have the same security base from which to operate as they did in the past incarnation. Often their status in life is and has been similar in so far as society deems such. Both persons have been practical, conservative men in a past life and are now bringing those vibrations into the present association. It will be difficult for either person to be subjected to the other's complete authority. Keywords are owner and banker, governor and senator, employer and manager, or guardian and father..

Saturn-Pluto
Both of these two individuals are strong and capable personalities accustomed to ruling their own destinies. Pluto forces long-term changes upon the Saturn person through reasoning and pressure. Saturn can respect Pluto's strength of character and arguments without being in complete agreement. Since Pluto is a generational force of change, this does not represent an intimate association between two souls who last related in male bodies. Keywords are senator and detective,

captain and mutineer, patriarch and innovator, aged man and plastic surgeon, statesman and assassin, or shepherd and mine owner.

Considering Uranus in Karmic Comparisons

Many people will resist anything new because they misunderstand the purpose of change. The world will soon diversify so that progress on all planes is realized. Uranus in the horoscope reveals the personal reaction to transformations. It says, "release the old and make room for the new if you are not afraid to do so."

Impersonal wisdom is developed over a long period of time through a variety of experiences. When Uranus can transcend personal desires and gains, he recognizes the soul value of every living thing. Then there is no fear, no intimate love, no possessiveness, and no judgment. In the wake of his seemingly disruptive action, Uranus brings the possibility of progress. So it is with the political rebels of both past and present. Their task is only to liberate society from all restrictive forms and systems in order for a new order to be established. Unfortunately, corrupt governments are usually replaced by equally tainted substitutes that merely have different names and titles. The real lesson is that freedom comes only through responsible action and after karmic duties are performed. Freedom is never personal, but universal.

In considering past incarnations, Uranus represents a masculine entity who is truly wiser than Saturn, although he appears in the guise of an adventurer or a revolutionary. This individual is quite different from the Mars warrior who is concerned only with personal desires and gain. The mature Uranus is as committed to obtaining freedom for others as for himself.

Keywords are astrologer, test pilot, anarchist, genius, scandalizer, union organizer, lawless one, rebel, futurist, engineer, astronaut, fanatic, scientist, proselytizer, eccentric, ecologist libertine, reformer, inventor, eccentric, alchemist, liberator, or electrician.

Uranus-Uranus
This contact is found between persons born within two or three years of each other and thus is more generational than personal. They were together during times of similar changes in the past explained by the zodiacal sign of the conjunction. Keywords are engineer and electrician, test pilot and astronaut, fanatic and rebel, or astrologer and alchemist.

Uranus-Ceres
The sensible Ceres person does not really like the Uranus individual who wants to upset her secure little domain. Ceres, who was a female servant or farm woman in the past life, thought that innovative Uranus, a former male rebel, wasted money and effort on his idealistic dreams of a future with equality for all. Keywords are Russian Bolshevik and manor servant, alchemist and village midwife, scientist and milkmaid, or astronaut and nurse.

Uranus-Pallas
Mental rapport is possible for these individuals because Pallas sees possibilities for implementing the ideas Uranus voices. These objective people enjoy brainstorming together even if the association goes no further. In the past incarna-

tion, female Pallas promoted opportunities for the male alchemist Uranus to prove his theories. Keywords are liberator and troop trainer, reformer and women's rights advocate, scientist and instructor, astrologer and counselor, or futurist and sculptress.

Uranus-Juno
Such an impractical man simply cannot give Juno the status and security she needs for happiness. No matter that Uranus was an innovative lover in the past life, the Juno former female scorns a permanent alliance again in this life. If these two individuals are bound together, there will be an abundance of nagging and complaining from both parties. Keywords are innovative lover and titled lady, rebel and queen, astrologer and wealthy widow, fanatic and practical housekeeper, or eccentric and proper hostess.

Uranus-Vesta
Uranus feels restricted when in the presence of Vesta because of her strict manner of living. The rules that Vesta willingly imposes upon herself make Uranus feel unreasonably bound. This combination is not good for a personal relationship. Uranus delights in shocking Vesta, the former celibate nun. Keywords are libertine and celibate nun, rebel and strict ritualist, fanatic and social woman, or astrologer and conservative housewife.

Uranus-Neptune
Persons having these planets in comparison conjunctions can develop a high degree of psychic attunement with each other. Because of the period of motion of both Uranus and Neptune, these contacts will involve groups rather than lone individuals. Keywords are reformer and clergyman, futurist and

71

dreamer, genius and magician, astrologer and medium, or ecologist and romantic.

Uranus-Pluto
These planets are both instruments of universal change, so individuals having this conjunction are once again living together during a period of worldwide transformation. The alterations may be political, social, economic, or spiritual, depending upon the time frames involved. Keywords are rebel and mutineer, innovator and refiner, anarchist and dictator, fanatic and gangster, or eccentric and psychologist.

Considering Neptune in Karmic Comparisons

Negatively, Neptune doesn't always play fair or accept his share of the blame for wrongdoings. Neptune can be the fool for both himself and associates when he glamorizes an ideal or goal for self-glory. And when that scheme backfires, the emotional Neptune person seeks some form of escape. Many past lives for Neptune individuals are as alcoholics who chose that means to escape.

On the positive side, Neptune can express faith and deep love for another who is completely undeserving of either emotion. There is absolute responsiveness to spiritual or psychic urges, disregarding all logical arguments against such actions. These are people who follow their dreams or their messages to either success or failure.

A Neptune soul may have incarnated in either a masculine or a feminine body during past lives. Because of the male dominance even in the religious vocations during recorded history, we usually think of priests, ministers, magicians, physicians, etc., as masculine. However, much of the vibration of Neptune involves a manifestation of the feminine principles of compassion, intuition, artistry, symbolism, healing, and response to inspiration.

Great musicians, dancers, actors and poets of the past may be represented by Neptune contacts in the horoscope. These people were able to express their inner visions in symbols or tones for all the world to share. Personal emotions were set aside to make room for cosmic experiences to be expanded. An elevation of Neptune represents complete surrender of human will.

Keywords are poet, mystic, medium, musician, dreamer, magician, chaplain, photographer, serenader, romantic, pessimist, troubadour, alcoholic, priest, witch doctor, ballet dancer, celibate monk, psychic, actor, healer, physician, a teller of tales or sage, trickster, or idealist.

Neptune-Neptune
Because of its motion, Neptune will be conjunct Neptune in all charts of persons born within three to five years of each other. This position of Neptunes conjunct shows either how groups of people were disillusioned in the past or where these individuals found their spiritual inspiration. Keywords are mystic and medium, poet and troubadour, priest and chaplain, healer and physician, or actor and illusionist.

Neptune-Ceres
The practical nature of Ceres makes her quite motherly with a confused Neptune. She will not be interested in following through on any of Neptune's dreams, but only in helping him

see reality. In several cases the former female, Ceres, cared for Neptune, the former alcoholic son or nephew, during a past incarnation. Keywords are mother and dreamer son, aunt and alcoholic nephew, nursemaid and young musician, or servant and poet.

Neptune-Pallas
Since Pallas is oriented toward productive activity, she will have only a fleeting interest in Neptune's dreams and schemes. In a past incarnation, the feminine Pallas weaver enjoyed the poignant music and songs of wandering minstrel Neptune, but was not drawn to his roving way of life. Keywords are alcoholic and counselor, troubadour and weaver, magician and guardsman, or chaplain and instructor.

Neptune-Juno
Oh, what tales Neptune did weave when first he began to deceive lovely lady Juno. In a past life the protected and snobbish Juno was completely taken in by the handsome rake Neptune. A real teller of tales was this courtly gentleman who was looking for an easy way to attract a fortune. That fear of deception remains with the Juno person to the present time when these two planets are conjunct. Keywords are queen and troubadour, woman and mystic, or hostess and alcoholic guest.

Neptune-Vesta
These two entities can either be quite compatible because of past lives serving in religious institutions, or be in conflict because Neptune refuses to follow the dictates of the prevailing moral system. Vesta, as a female nun or temple server in a past incarnation, is accustomed to following the priestly Neptune's directions so long as he does not vary from the for-

mula set up by their superiors. In that case, Vesta will be very disappointed in Neptune's failures. Keywords are priest and nun, dreamer and idealist, mystic and druid, monk and nun, or servers of the same temple.

Neptune-Pluto
The conjunction will occur rarely in time because of the slow motion of Neptune and Pluto. Individuals involved have lived through tumultuous changes in the past and will do so once again. Keywords are priest and dictator, dreamer and assassin, witch doctor and psychologist, or musician and guru.

Considering Pluto in Karmic Comparisons

During the 1930s, when Pluto was located and named, the world was in a period of tumult and upheaval. There was violence in the streets, mobsters were taking over America's cities, peasants and noblemen alike were starving in Russia, despots ruled Central and South America with iron fists, fanaticism was rising in Germany as Hitler came to power, and the world was in the throes of a severe economic depression. It is no wonder that contemporary astrologers looked upon this new planet Pluto as the symbol of coercion and violence.

In reality, Pluto is a transmitter of universal evolution on many levels. This energy is like a great moving glacier that slowly but surely remodels the land over which it slides inch by inch. The old systems and values must be set aside willingly or forcefully to make room for a new order. This has been true since the world began. On a personal scale this can be likened to the habitual emptying of the bowel to make room for more food each day, or else the body stagnates and becomes ill. Another example in nature is the Dead Sea, where waters flow in but there is no outlet to complete the cycle. Thus, this body of water holds its salinity while the fresh waters evaporate, leaving a place where no life can exist. Pluto is a symbol of necessary evacuation, regardless of the pain of the process.

On this same level is the concept of Pluto as both the symbol of procreation and death. Without a balance of souls and bodies incarnating during any period of history, there would be too many physical demands for the planet to fill and then all life would cease. Pluto is really the universal juggler of need and availability. When man does not comply willingly, he is forced into action for the benefit of humanity as an incarnating race. "Release of all personal impulses so that life can go forth" is the message of Pluto.

Keywords are undertaker, detective, occultist, dictator, propagandist, occultist, assassin, nightmare, psychologist, mutineer, transformer, gangster, kidnapper, guru, lover, plastic surgeon, oil refiner, mine operator, war chief, or despot.

How Does the Past Affect the Future?

By looking at a few example chart comparisons of actual clients, it is possible to show how the past life influences come up in present day relationships.

In Chart 4, the following planets are considered to be effective in the karmic comparison:

Male	to	Female	in	Sign
Pluto	to	Pluto	in	Gemini
Venus	to	Jupiter	in	Sagittarius
Moon	to	Vesta	in	Virgo/Libra

This husband and wife have very few interests in common and spend little time together. Their lack of many planets conjunct in the karmic comparison suggests that they have not had numerous previous incarnations in close association.

Their Plutos are within the five-degree orb allowed saying that these two individuals have lived in group situations be-

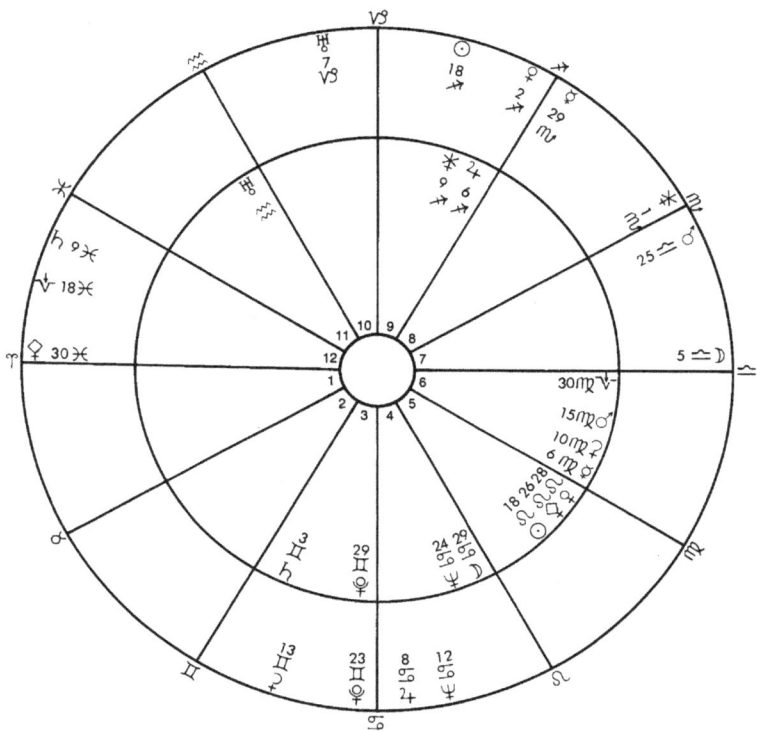

Chart 4. A: inner, female; B: outer, male

fore. With Pluto in Gemini, they probably lived near the end of the Age of Chivalry when the romantic days filled with tournaments and feasting gave way to more realistic times. This couple does enjoy traveling together.

The man's Moon is in an out-of-sign conjunction with his wife's Vesta. The Vesta influence is strongly brought to the fore because she is a practicing occultist who spends much time in meditation and study while the husband gladly cares for the housework and chores. In this age they are repeating a life as mother and priestess daughter. Because of the crossing over of the two signs, that previous life was probably in India around the time of the conquests of Alexander the Great. The influx of Grecian soldiers brought long-lasting changes to northern and central India during that period around 300 B.C.

A further contact betweeri the man's Venus and the woman's Jupiter show a life when their present sexual roles were re-versed. The present husband was a lovely young lady in early Japan when the present wife was an older, more sophisti-cated government official. They were married according to 'Parental wishes and lived a formal, but social. existence. One of the few things the couple enjoy together in present days is entertaining friends and relatives.

During the incarnation together, these two individuals are just beginning to learn to relate as a loving husband and wife, and having difficulty with any displays of affection to each other. They respect and admire each other for various accom-plishments, but live in the same house more as compatible strangers than sweethearts.

In Chart 5, the following planets are considered to be effec-tive in the karmic comparisons:

Male	to	Female	in	Sign
Saturn	to	Ceres	in	Aries
Sun	to	Uranus	in	Leo
Sun	to	Moon	in	Leo
Jupiter	to	Moon	in	Leo
Mars	to	Neptune	in	Scorpio

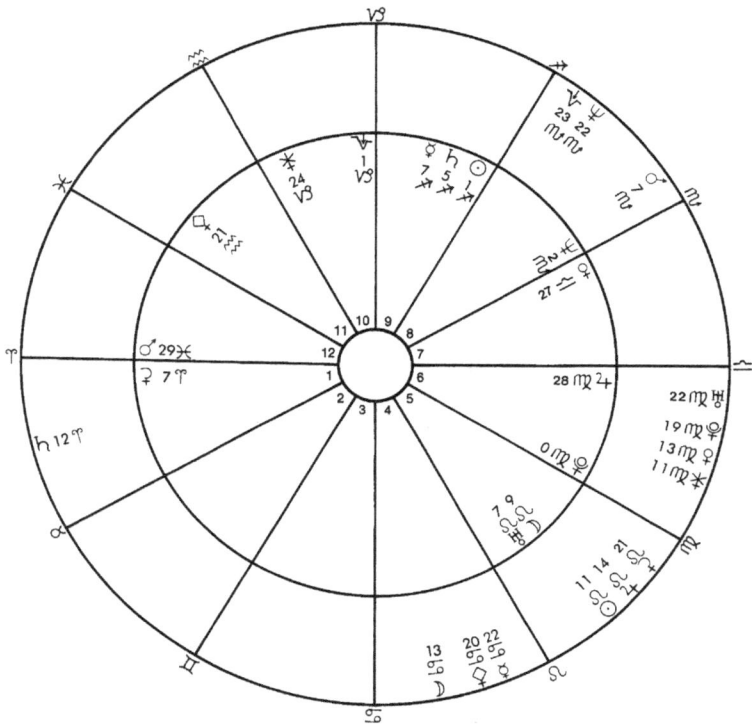

Chart 5. A: inner, female; B: outer, male

This chart comparison is between a brother and sister who are widely separated by years, but very closely tied emotionally. From the time her baby brother was born, this freedom-loving tomboy dictated what would be done for the child.

There is no doubt in either present day parent's mind that the girl cared for the present day brother on the forty-year trek across the desert with Moses of biblical times. Her maternal Ceres conjunct the boy's Saturn in Aries shows both the time period and the nurturing relationship. During that previous sojourn, both entities were an older couple or aging siblings who fed and cared for one another during trying times. Though not Jewish, both the boy and girl are more drawn to Jewish friends and cultural activities than their own religious affiliations.

The brother's Sun in Leo is conjunct both Uranus and Moon in his sister's natal horoscope, indicating two past lives where he held sway over her. In all probability, the Sun-Uranus connection indicates a life in the Egypt of pyramid builders when the boy was a major or minor ruler with his scientific sister serving, then in a male body, as a favored court astrologer or engineer. They have respected each other's opinions and rights since babyhood, with none of the usual sibling squabbles.

Because the boy's Sun is closely linked to this sister's Moon, these two individuals are candidates for having been born previously as brother and sister who were slated for a royal marriage, making them co-rulers in an ancient land. There are no incestuous shadows on the present relationship because of the great difference in age, but each shows an abiding love and concern for the other. There is a tendency to measure prospective dates and mates against sibling, rather than parental prototypes.

Jupiter of the male's natal chart conjunct Moon of the female's horoscope brings yet another life of worshipful pride into the complex scheme of these intertwined lives. Whether these entities lived as wedded spouses or were proud mother and adored son has not been determined. Neither is there sufficient evidence to understand the need of the girl to always provide the best of gifts and care for her younger sibling. She checks to be sure the parents are being generous enough with him. This past life was in the time of Louis XIV of France.

The tie of Mars in the male horoscope to Neptune in the female's indicates desire to follow in his sister's footsteps in so far as is possible. He cannot always understand her idealism, but would die trying to protect her. The brother is interested in sports and military activity, while the sister is quite philosophical around him. She retains her former role as chaplain-confessor to the past life soldier who is now her little brother.

Keyword Guide

Sun: father, husband, boss, ruler, authority figure. knight, lord of the castle, master. governor, executive. guardian, employer. manager, powerful ally, and ship captain

Sun-Sun: co-rulers, equal males, allies, or foes

Sun-Moon: husband and wife, king and queen, man and woman, or brother and sister

Sun-Mercury: ruler and student, knight and squire, hero and admirer, star and fan, king and clown, editor and reporter, publisher and author, or principal and teacher

Sun-Venus: master and maiden, man and mistress, king and concubine, wanderer and enchantress, giver and receiver of gifts, lord and entertainer, mandarin and geisha, buyer and lingerie saleslady, or gentleman and nail technician

Sun-Mars: captain and soldier, man and youth, leader and worker. dean and student, sergeant and enlistee, king and guard, trainer and slave, or guard and prisoner

Sun-Ceres: heir and doting mother or aunt, prince and nanny,

landlord and tenant, adored grandson and grandmother, lord and maid servant, or knight and serf

Sun-Pallas: boss and employee, chairman and secretary, diplomat and interpreter, noted author and editor, politician and interviewer, president and speech writer, or
plantation owner and overseer

Sun-Juno: husband and wife, lord and lady of the manor, man
and nagging wife, provider and sponge, sire and
mother of his children, suitor and frigid maiden, king
and queen, or corpse and widow

Sun-Vesta: chaplain and nun, pope and mother superior,
pimp and prostitute, hero and worshiper, adored one
and caretaker, or husband and obsessed wife

Sun-Jupiter: man and professor, leader and supporter, cultural and social equals, two philosophers, author and
critic, host and snob, king and counselor, monarch
and archbishop, hero and proud friend, executive and
confidante, or prince and advisor.

Sun-Saturn: prince and tutor, man and father, student and
teacher, general and commander, hero and jealous
old man, criminal and jailer, lord of the castle and
leader of siege forces, captain and owner of line, husband and father-in-law, or president and chairman of
the board

Sun-Uranus: ruler and court astrologer, commander and test
pilot, king and anarchist, executive and genius, lord
and rebel, or master and lawless one

Sun-Neptune: king and priest, ruler and religious advisor,
lord of manor and monk, knight and minstrel, man
and healer, querent and medium, patient and prayer

leader, captain and sage, or guardian and liar

Sun-Pluto: prince and dictator, ruler and assassin, man and childhood nightmares, executive and psychologist, or captain and mutineer

Moon: mother, wife, medium, cook, sailor, receptive person, female, opinionated, domestic, family interests, martyr, or woman

Moon-Moon: co-wives, sisters, like-minded females, harem dwellers, or cousins

Moon-Mercury: mother and child, cook and maid, restaurant owner and waitress, lady and squire, two friends of different ages

Moon-Venus: sister and sister, mother and beautiful daughter, wife and mistress, woman and dance instructor, matron and cosmetologist, spouse and sister-in-law, female and photographer, friendly women

Moon-Mars: mother and soldier son, woman and flirtatious man, doting mother and rebellious son, possessive woman and male relative, female and carpenter, queen and guardsman, or maiden and abductor

Moon-Ceres: mother and nursemaid, woman and nurse, woman and servant, housekeeper and produce farmer, female and stepmother, princess and godmother, or orphan girl and foster mother

Moon-Pallas: mother and career woman, wife and husband's assistant, older female and young office worker, woman and accountant, or aunt and niece

Moon-Juno: mother and lovely daughter, woman and lady of the manor, queen and lady in waiting, woman and seamstress, mother-in-law and insecure wife, or woman and social superior

Moon-Vesta: mother and nun, bereaved wife and priestess, old woman and unmarried daughter, abandoned woman and social worker, loving mama and delicate daughter, or religious women

Moon-Jupiter: mother and priest son, mother and philosopher, widow and adored only son, female and benefactor, matriarch and counselor, or queen and social equal

Moon-Saturn: woman and elderly father, female and banker, maiden and guardian, woman and jailer, mother and scholarly son, widow and eldest child, or female student and professor

Moon-Uranus: woman and innovative teacher, female and astrologer, queen and advisor, mother and engineer son, maiden and rebel, or woman and scientist

Moon-Neptune: queen and teacher of religion, woman and chaplain, female and deceiving lover, wife and thief, lovely maiden and serenader, female and sailor, or woman and priest brother

Moon-Pluto: queen and assassin, female and dictator, mother and gangster son, woman and kidnapper, maid and guru, or gypsy wife and lover

Mercury: art or drama critic, linguist, student, script writer, traveler, signer for the deaf, reader for the blind, messenger, author, orator, scribe, squire, thinker, reporter; sibling, media commentator, communications specialist, or guide

Mercury-Mercury: children of same parents, live in same

home, students in classroom, friends, reporters, or media consultants and employees

Mercury-Venus: child and big sister, critic and artist, teenager and cosmetologist, youth and beauty queen, script writer, or friends

Mercury-Mars: youth and petty criminal, file clerk and police officer, sibling and big brother, teacher and boisterous student, recruit and soldier, or debater

Mercury-Ceres: child and nanny, file clerk and nurse, volunteer and hospital administrator, traveler and guide, squire and housemaid

Mercury-Pallas: student and instructor, handicraft worker and instructor, radio commentator and female politician, student and riding teacher, messenger and executive assistant

Mercury-Juno: flower girl and bride, writer and matron, reporter and society leader, companion and lady, or speaker and patroness

Mercury-Vesta: child and nun, signer and deaf person, novice and mother superior, neophyte and temple server, or girl and older sister

Mercury-Jupiter: child and minister, student and professor, critic and publisher, linguist and traveler, squire and king's counselor, orator and promoter, client and lawyer, or reporter and editor

Mercury-Saturn: truant and jailer, student and principal, adult and aged parent, file clerk and employer, or reporter and governor

Mercury-Uranus: novice and fanatic, recruit and proselytizer, student and rebel, or reporter and dictator

Mercury-Neptune: typist and poet, squire and chaplain, child and photographer, student and magician, client and medium, or penitent parishioner and priest

Mercury-Pluto: recruit and rebel, student and occultist, youth and speaker on reincarnation, or reporter and political reformer

Venus: artist, singer, dancer, party giver, joyous female, acknowledged beauty, young woman, sympathizer, beautician, manicurist, model, fashion plate, dieter, mistress, or indolent woman

Venus-Venus: sisters, women friends, members of same ballet troupe, choir members, performers of piano duets, partners in beauty venture, or jewelers.

Venus-Mars: lovers, wife and husband, mother and father of young family, mistress and lover, woman and man, or lady and knight

Venus-Ceres: wife and farmer, lady and nanny, girl and stepmother, daughter and mother, orphan and custodian, patient and nurse, or mistress and maid

Venus-Pallas: shopper and silversmith, artist and supplier of paints, mistress and skilled female worker, model and instructor or housewife and interior decorator

Venus-Juno: mistress and wife, competitors, woman and dressmaker, ballerina and patroness of arts, or mourner and widow

Venus-Vesta: laywoman and nun, or matron and temple priestess

Venus-Jupiter: flirt and government official, woman and

man, beauty queen and professor, divorced woman and lawyer, or mistress and lover

Venus-Saturn: lovely lady and strict teacher, woman and aged father, dancer and choreographer, romanticist and realist, or wife and older husband

Venus-Uranus: lady and mad scientist, mistress and passionate lover, female and political radical, singer and eccentric musician, or wife and abductor

Venus-Neptune: woman and priest, disciple and master, female assistant and magician, famous beauty and poet, or wife and unfaithful husband

Venus-Pluto: dieter and resort manager, renowned beauty and plastic surgeon, model and fashion designer, or investor and banker

Mars: young man, soldier, sports figure, surgeon, gladiator, dentist, carpenter, warrior, swordsman, militia, worker, machinist, train engineer, primitive tribesman, Native American brave, hunter, guard, petty criminal, laborer, courageous youth, or barber

Mars-Mars: mortal enemies, soldier and soldier, Native American brave and warrior, machinist and worker, fencer and swordsman, or two wrestlers

Mars-Ceres: boy and nursemaid, warrior and healer, carpenter and housemaid, surgeon and nurse, brave and herbalist, or hunter and dresser of hides

Mars-Pallas: swordsman and fencing instructor, criminal and social worker, gladiator and trainer, or knight and horse trainer

Mars-Juno: husband and wife, soldier and lady of the manor,

guard and queen, rapist and female victim, petty criminal and wealthy homeowner, murderer and widow of victim, or explorer and vigilant wife

Mars-Vesta: brave and medicine woman, active young man and meditator, crusader and religious celibate, soldier and pacifist, or extrovert and introvert

Mars-Jupiter: soldier and philosopher, young man and older playboy, carpenter and architect, bus driver and traveler, waiter and gourmet, guard and wealthy homeowner, or sports professional and financial backer

Mars-Saturn: son and father, warrior and chieftain, criminal and jailer, boy and disciplinarian, or titled gentleman and his heir

Mars-Uranus: soldier and rebel, campaigner and politician, machinist and engineer, hunter and ecologist, laborer and scientist, or youth and libertine

Mars-Neptune: surgeon and pharmacist, warrior and dreamer, tribesman and witch doctor, sports figure and ballet dancer, or lover and celibate monk

Mars-Pluto: police officer and detective, laborer and oil refiner, miner and mine operator, or warrior and war chief

Jupiter: minister, physician, lawyer, philanthropist, prophet, guru, professor, traveler, sportsman, horseback rider, editor, publisher, friend of the family, patron of the arts, or social elitist.

Jupiter-Jupiter: rector and rabbi, fellow travelers, patron of the symphony and backer of the ballet, host and happy guest, editor and publisher, director and producer, or prophet and guru

Jupiter-Ceres: wealthy man and maidservant, joyful father and nanny, physician and nurse, or honored professor and farm woman

Jupiter-Pallas: proud father and professional daughter, art patron and talented weaver, member of the hunt and horse trainer, professor and assistant, traveler and interpreter, or minister and assistant

Jupiter-Juno: financier and treasurer of the board, husband and wife, philanthropist and patroness of the arts, or king and queen

Jupiter-Vesta: chaplain and nun, minister and Altar Guild volunteer, or guru and disciple

Jupiter-Saturn: social leader and puritan, spendthrift and miser, Liberal and Tory, rabbi and president of the congregation, rector and bishop, or president of company and chairman of board

Jupiter-Uranus: absent-minded professor and scientist, prince and union organizer, politician and rebel, or conservative publisher and scandal sheet editor

Jupiter-Neptune: minister and chaplain, optimist and pessimist, director and actor, patron and musician, physician and healer, or gentleman and troubadour

Jupiter-Pluto: lawyer and lobbyist, clergyman and social worker, philosopher and psychiatrist, or traveler and immigration official

Saturn: older person, rigid or responsible man, patriarch, governor, principal, employer, statesman, shepherd, conservative, father, disciplinarian, chairman of the board, grandfather, Father Time, jailer, owner, eldest son, or realist

Saturn-Saturn: owner and banker, governor and senator, employer and manager, or guardian and father

Saturn-Ceres: elderly man and nurse, landowner and gleaner, grandfather and grandmother, governor and maidservant, or dean of male students and dean of female students

Saturn-Pallas: proud grandfather and successful granddaughter, patriarch and fine weaver, statesman and ombudswoman, governor and captain of horse guard, or employer and thrifty employee

Saturn-Juno: old man and expensive young wife, corpse and weeping widow, governor and official hostess, patriarch and daughter-in-law, or harem owner and favorite concubine

Saturn-Vesta: old man and his celibate sister, guardian and wayward orphan, patriarch and temple priestess, eldest son and keeper of father's grave, realist and idealist, or conservative man and social wife

Saturn-Uranus: scholar and genius, employer and innovator, statesman and rebel, disciplinarian and fanatic, president and anarchist, or shepherd and ecologist

Saturn-Neptune: realist and dreamer, father and roving sailor, statesman and troubadour, jailer and alcoholic, employer and moody worker, or grandfather and actor

Saturn-Pluto: senator and detective, captain and mutineer, patriarch and innovator, aged man and plastic surgeon, statesman and assassin, or shepherd and mine owner

Uranus: astrologer, test pilot, anarchist, genius, scandalizer, union organizer, lawless one, rebel, futurist, engineer, astronaut, fanatic, scientist, proselytizer, eccentric, ecologist, libertine, reformer, inventor, eccentric, alchemist, liberator, or electrician

Uranus-Uranus: engineer and electrician, test pilot and astronaut, fanatic and rebel, or astrologer and alchemist

Uranus-Ceres: Russian Bolshevik and manor servant, alchemist and village midwife, scientist and milkmaid, or astronaut and nurse

Uranus-Pallas: liberator and troop trainer, reformer and women's rights advocate, scientist and instructor, astrologer and counselor, or futurist and sculptress

Uranus-Juno: innovative lover and titled lady, rebel and queen, astrologer and wealthy widow, fanatic and practical housekeeper, or eccentric and proper hostess

Uranus-Vesta: libertine and celibate nun, rebel and strict ritualist, fanatic and social woman, or astrologer and conservative housewife

Uranus-Neptune: reformer and clergyman, futurist and dreamer, genius and magician, astrologer and medium, or ecologist and romantic

Uranus-Pluto: rebel and mutineer, innovator and refiner, anarchist and dictator, fanatic and gangster, or eccentric and psychologist

Neptune: poet, mystic, medium, musician, dreamer, magician, chaplain, photographer, serenader, romantic, pessimist, troubadour, alcoholic, priest, witch doctor, ballet dancer, celibate monk, psychic, actor, healer, physician, a teller of tales, trickster, or idealist

Neptune-Neptune: mystic. and medium, poet and troubadour, priest and chaplain, healer and physician, or
actor and illusionist

Neptune-Ceres: mother and dreamer son, aunt and alcoholic nephew, nursemaid and young magician, or
servant and poet

Neptune-Pallas: alcoholic and counselor, troubadour and
weaver, magician and guardsman, or chaplain and
instructor

Neptune-Juno: vain courtier and princess, queen and troubadour, woman and mystic, or hostess and alcoholic guest

Neptune-Vesta: priest and nun, dreamer and idealist, mystic and druid, monk and nun, or servers of the same
temple

Neptune-Pluto: priest and dictator, dreamer and assassin,
witch doctor and psychologist, or musician and
mutineer

Pluto: occultist, detective, dictator, assassin, nightmare,
psychologist, mutineer, gangster, kidnapper, guru,
lover, plastic surgeon, oil refiner, mine operator or
owner, or war chief

www.ingramcontent.com/pod-product-compliance
Lightning Source LLC
Chambersburg PA
CBHW022029090426

42739CB00006BA/346